PRAISE FOR

"Guys: Don't let her know you are reading this book. Just read it, do it, and watch her attitude change. It's practical, easy to read, and extremely helpful. I highly recommend it."

—GARY CHAPMAN, PhD
AUTHOR OF *THE FIVE LOVE LANGUAGES*

"I once spoke at an event where only seven people showed up. Why? Because Doug Fields was in the next room, absolutely killing it! I wanted to be in that room, listening along with everyone else. In a world that often rewards quiet, gray lives, it's great to know Doug is living a bold life and a brave marriage and calling us to do the same."

—JON ACUFF
NEW YORK TIMES BEST-SELLING AUTHOR OF
START AND *STUFF CHRISTIANS LIKE*

"There are very few marriage books written for men. Doug Fields hits a grand slam with great words of wisdom, written in a most enjoyable way. Doug understands the joys and frustrations of what men are going through, plus he is really fun to read."

—DR. KEVIN LEMAN
NEW YORK TIMES BEST-SELLING AUTHOR OF
SHEET MUSIC AND *HAVE A NEW HUSBAND BY FRIDAY*

"Every husband needs to read this book. We mean it! It will revolutionize your marriage. Not only that—you'll love Doug's writing. It's real, it's funny, it's vulnerable, it's grounded, and it's immeasurably practical. So what are you waiting for? If you're a guy and you're married, become your wife's hero starting right now by reading this book."

—DRS. LES AND LESLIE PARROTT
AUTHORS OF *SAVING YOUR MARRIAGE BEFORE IT STARTS*

"I train every day to be a world champion fighter, but I also need training and tips on how to be a better husband. Doug Fields provided those, and I'm planning on putting them into action and becoming my wife's hero."

—MARK MUNOZ
UFC TOP MIDDLEWEIGHT CONTENDER

"Doug Fields is one of America's finest communicators. This book helped me and will help every man I know become a better husband. He is practical, funny, challenging, and plus, he lives what he writes. I hope not only men read it but every men's group in America goes through it. It's perfect for group format."

—JIM BURNS, PHD
PRESIDENT, HOMEWORD, AND AUTHOR OF *CREATING AN INTIMATE MARRIAGE* AND *CONFIDENT PARENTING*

"Men, you will be seen as Mr. Wonderful if you take Doug Fields's words to heart. Doug knows his stuff. This book will grab your attention, you will learn a ton, and you won't have to figure out how to split the atom to do it. Plus, he's funny and transparent about his own marital missteps. You will walk away deeply encouraged as you realize that being a hero is less about scaling skyscrapers and more about brushing the dirt off your cape and flying again."

—SHAUNTI AND JEFF FELDHAHN
BEST-SELLING AUTHORS OF *FOR MEN ONLY: A STRAIGHTFORWARD GUIDE TO THE INNER LIVES OF WOMEN*

"I loved this book. It offers humorous, down-to-earth, straight talk for guys who want to be extraordinary lovers of their wives. If your personality profile is ESPN, you're willing to kill the bug for the woman you love, and you care about your sex life, this book is for you. So settle into your man-cave recliner and start reading."

—RON L. DEAL
SPEAKER, THERAPIST, AND BEST-SELLING
AUTHOR OF *THE SMART STEPFAMILY*

"This book is like weaponized uranium for married men. Put it into the heart of a man and watch out, ladies! I witnessed firsthand the laughing, the learning, and Doug's famous laser-guided missiles of truth hitting their marks and changing marriages before my eyes. The outcomes did it for me. In man-world *7 Ways to Be Her Hero* is the P90X of marriage material for men. You can simply stop all the guessing and start getting results fast. Your *before* and *after* snapshots will be shocking."

—KENNY LUCK

MEN'S EXPERT, AUTHOR OF *SLEEPING GIANT*, AND
PRESIDENT AND FOUNDER OF EVERY MAN MINISTRIES

"Doug is one of the most brilliant and relevant voices of our day and for generations to come. His amazing ability to communicate truth is present in his most recent book on marriage. *7 Ways to Be Her Hero* is one of the few marriage books that can make a difference in *your* marriage."

—STEVE ARTERBURN

AUTHOR, SPEAKER, COUNSELOR, RADIO TALK-SHOW
HOST OF *NEW LIFE LIVE!*, AND FOUNDER OF NEW
LIFE MINISTRIES AND WOMEN OF FAITH®

"*7 Ways to Be Her Hero* is a long-needed resource to help men understand what is expected of them, and now there is no excuse for a guy saying, 'I don't know what to do!' Every marriage needs a husband who has read and implemented what is contained inside!"

—DAVID STOOP, PHD

PSYCHOLOGIST AND COAUTHOR OF *JUST US:*
FINDING INTIMACY WITH GOD AND EACH OTHER

"Most of us men identify with wanting to achieve something heroic. Mostly, we assume this will happen in the marketplace or some other *out-there* arena. But what better or more fruitful place to be heroic than in our own marriages? Doug Fields comes alongside us with personal and professional credibility, offering practical, profoundly simple, and lighthearted counsel in *7 Ways to Be Her Hero*. Read it . . . if you dare!"

—ALAN FADLING

AUTHOR OF *AN UNHURRIED LIFE* AND
EXECUTIVE DIRECTOR OF THE LEADERSHIP INSTITUTE

"Even if you don't feel like you are hero material, you still need to read this book. It will give you hope and practical ideas on how to be a better husband. Doug Fields has a passion to help men win with their marriages. His writing will move you to take bold steps in doing the one thing that you can do better than any other man—be the kind of husband your wife needs. If you've ever struggled to find a model you can follow as a husband, here is a practical guide to help coach you."

—REGGIE JOINER
CEO AND FOUNDER OF ORANGE

"In terms of look, feel, language, and approach, most marriage books are geared for women. Not this one! It is unapologetically targeting the heart, mind, and experiences of men. This book is going to be a game-changer for many marriages. It has already made a difference in mine!"

—TED LOWE
FOUNDER OF MARRIEDPEOPLE

"Doug Fields invites you to experience the ultimate in your marriage and replaces the myth of marriage being a 50/50 equation with it being a 100/100 exchange. He reminds his male readers that love never gives up and to love their wives just as Christ loved the church. The authenticity of the author's own marriage is reflected in the pages of this book."

—JON WALLACE, DBA
PRESIDENT OF AZUSA PACIFIC UNIVERSITY

"My first thought upon reading Doug Fields's *7 Ways to Be Her Hero: The One Your Wife Has Been Waiting For* was, *Dang—that was pretty good!* It's full of good, commonsense ideas that are presented in the way the average guy probably hasn't seen before but will be glad he finally has. Want a better marriage? Check out this book now!"

—RICK JOHNSON
BEST-SELLING AUTHOR OF *BECOMING YOUR SPOUSE'S BETTER HALF* AND *HOW TO TALK SO YOUR HUSBAND WILL LISTEN AND LISTEN SO YOUR HUSBAND WILL TALK*

7

WAYS TO BE HER

HERO

THE ONE YOUR WIFE HAS
BEEN WAITING FOR

———— ————

DOUG FIELDS

W Publishing Group

An Imprint of Thomas Nelson

Published in Nashville, Tennessee, by W Publishing, an imprint of Thomas Nelson.

Published in association with the literary agency of WordServe Literary Group, Ltd., 10152 S. Knoll Circle, Highlands Ranch, Colorado 80130.

Thomas Nelson titles may be purchased in bulk for educational, business, fund-raising, or sales promotional use. For information, please e-mail SpecialMarkets@ThomasNelson.com.

Unless otherwise noted, Scripture quotations are taken from the Holy Bible, New International Version®, NIV®. © 1973, 1978, 1984, 2011 by Biblica, Inc.™ Used by permission of Zondervan. All rights reserved worldwide.

Scripture quotations marked NLT are taken from the *Holy Bible*, New Living Translation. © 1996, 2004, 2007 by Tyndale House Foundation. Used by permission of Tyndale House Publishers, Inc., Carol Stream, Illinois 60188. All rights reserved.

Scripture quotations marked CEV are taken from the Contemporary English Version. © 1991 by the American Bible Society. Used by permission.

Scripture quotations marked MSG are taken from *The Message* by Eugene H. Peterson. © 1993, 1994, 1995, 1996, 2000, 2001, 2002. Used by permission of NavPress Publishing Group. All rights reserved.

Scripture quotations marked ESV are taken from the English Standard Version. © 2001 by Crossway Bibles, a division of Good News Publishers.

Library of Congress Cataloging-in-Publication Data

Fields, Doug, 1962-
    7 ways to be her hero : the one your wife has been waiting for / Doug Fields.
        pages cm
    Includes bibliographical references.
    ISBN 978-0-8499-2056-1 (trade paper)
    1. Marriage—Religious aspects—Christianity. 2. Man-woman relationships—Religious aspects—Christianity. 3. Married people—Psychology. I. Title. II. Title: Seven ways to be her hero.
    BV4596.M3F54 2014
    248.8'425—dc23
                                        2013047888

Printed in the United States of America

14 15 16 17 18 RRD 6 5 4 3 2 1

Cathy Fields

You make it so easy to want to be a great husband!

I wish I could capture all that you are and all that you do and put it into words—those principles could change so many marriages around the world.

You are the most amazing human I know, and the thought of spending another thirty years together brings me such great joy!

Thank you for being the inspiration to the words in this book.

CONTENTS

ACKNOWLEDGMENTS

Almost everything I have ever done in my life that has any useful value has fastened itself to the help of others. The writing of this book has been no exception. During the eighteen months I toiled with this content—first speaking it, then writing, tweaking, conversing, testing, and writing some more—so many people contributed in instrumental roles. And this is my opportunity to express my gratefulness.

First and foremost is my mentor, friend, hero, coworker, and biggest cheerleader, Jim Burns. Much of who I am today points back to this amazing man who I profoundly love. I am also indebted to Jim Liebelt and Greg Johnson (my amazing literary agent) who read and re-read every word and came to my rescue when I said, "I need a better way to say this . . ." Their giftedness appears throughout this book.

I tend to hide when I write, but my friends don't seem to like that about the writing process, and they leaned in with their friendship and displayed it in unique and personal ways. I am blessed to have so many friends, but these guys poured it on during this writing process: Seth Bartlette, Sandy Boyd, Fadi Cheikha, David Dendy, Josh Griffin, Dan Hamer, Charlie

Koeller, Jeff Maguire, Matt McGill, Jay Miller, Chris Reed, Duffy Robbins, Steve Rutenbar, Tim Timmons (Jr. and Sr.), Greg Vujnov, and Doug Webster. Your roles in my life can't be expressed in words!

I am also very thankful to Pete and Sandy Jones for taking a risk and opening a CrossFit Gym, which has become a place of escape for me to be refreshed physically so I'm stronger in other areas of my life as well—I have deep gratitude to both of you.

Almost every day I wake up thinking of our many DYM-members (downloadyouthministry.com), most of whom I don't know personally, but I know what you do every week, and I am inspired by your commitment to help young people become heroes of their faith. I love thinking of ways to serve you and make your job easier.

As for my paying job, the people I work with at The HomeWord Center for Youth & Family at Azusa Pacific University are audacious enough to believe we can change the world of marriage, family, parenting, and leadership. The behind the scenes folks are Andrew Accardy, Dr. Dave Bixby, Randy Bramel, Becca Burns, Dean Bruns, Rod Emery, Bob Howard, Shawn King, David Lane, Tom Mitchell, Dr. David Peck, Debbie Pflieger, Tom Purcell, Krista Salazar, Ken Verheyen, Dr. Jon Wallace, and Cindy Ward, who can be found cheering on this dream!

Often during this writing process, I found myself capturing stories from the people I had the privilege to serve for thirty years at both Mariners' and Saddleback Church, and those relationships continue to inspire and fuel me. It was the leadership of Kenny Luck and Rick Warren, who invited me to teach this material to their men's groups, that started this whole project—I love and appreciate both of you.

Lastly, everything in my life circles back to my family—I consider myself most blessed that God would reward us by adding a couple extra children for Cathy and I to love as our own: Delia Baltierra and Kevin and Lindsey Cram (and baby Cohen), thank you for expanding and enriching our lives. As I wrote this book, I thought deeply of my own children, Torie, Cody, and Cassie, three of the most amazing young adults the world has seen. May the words in this book be a reflection to you of how much I love your mom and how I want your future marriages to be overflowing with health. I love you deeply and am honored to be your dad.

START HERE

This is a book intended for men. I am guessing some women will sneak around and read it (and will most definitely get something out of it). For this I apologize in advance. I am not sure exactly what I am apologizing for, but as a husband for thirty years, I have lived long enough to know that at times, a man's best course of action is to simply, and quickly, apologize to women. Consider it done. Again, I am sorry. Very sorry.

Because my primary audience for this book is guys (sorry, sneaky ladies), I am writing in a way that *most men* seem to talk and learn. Some women likely will not understand my humor or word choice and will simply dismiss me for being crude. I am not writing to be crude; I simply use some terms and phrases that are *guy-isms* in an attempt to reach and connect with men. And if you are a guy who does not agree with the way I portray how most men think, then I apologize to you too. But you must know, I spend *a lot* of time speaking to men's groups, hanging with guys, and I know most guys will *get it* and laugh, which makes my incredible life-changing thoughts and inspirational truths a little easier to digest. (Hyperbole included, courtesy of my editor.)

Many authors would not get away with this many guy-isms. I want to thank W Publishing Group, my publisher, for having the courage to let me write to men the way most men talk and think. They did not let me be as gratuitous as I wanted, but I think it still speaks the way men like. (FYI: If you are the ultra-conservative type, this may not be the book for you.)

7 Ways to Be Her Hero: The One Your Wife Has Been Waiting For is not my original title. I wanted to call it *How Not to Suck as a Husband.* But then, I knew, men would not think it was believable since we know we all suck to varying degrees of "suckiness." Then I thought about using the title *How to Get All the Sex You Want,* which is quite an eye-catching title, if I do say so myself. But the reality is that most guys do not buy books. Frankly, most guys do not even read books; we read magazines. Actually, we don't even read magazines; we browse through them, looking at pictures. We may read an online article if there is the potential for something to explode or to learn a new tidbit on sex. Women read books. Women buy books. So I decided that if there was any hope of your wife buying this book and setting it by the toilet for you to peruse, the title *How to Get All the Sex You Want* probably would not work with a female book-buying audience (although I bet if you applied a lot of what I talk about in this book, you would get a lot more sex—but that is not scientifically verifiable).

7 Ways to Be Her Hero is really what the book is about. It is a pretty fitting title, too, because most husbands want to be heroic at *something.* High school or college sports are long gone. We are not hitting walk-off homers in the majors as we had dreamed. We haven't hit a game-winning three-pointer since grade school (even in our imaginations). And the most heroic thing most of us did in football was either try out for the team or limit our concussions to three.

Marriage is work, sure. But by the end of our lives, we will be glad we can know we were our brides' occasional heroes and that we tried our best. And that is a key theme of a hero. He tries. More on that later. Back to sucking as a man.

I have a pastor-friend who was approached by a forty-year-old guy asking to be baptized. My buddy questioned him, "Why do you want to be baptized?" The guy proudly proclaimed, "I just don't want to suck anymore!" This is the cry of so many men. We know we suck, and we don't want to suck anymore. This is especially true when it comes to marriage (and to parenting—but that is another book for another time).

For most guys, a lot of their life-domains are going well . . . except for their marriages. They will say, "My job is going fine. My health is adequate. My fantasy football team came in second place last season. The kids haven't died on my watch (yet). But truth be told . . . I'm *not* a very good husband."

Yes, it takes two to make a great marriage, no denying that. For a marriage to really zing, both husband and wife have to be *all in*. But there is only one person on the planet you really have the power to change: you. And addressing this issue is the heart of this book. Helping guys become less-sucky husbands is one of the passions of my own heart. I am really excited for you to digest this book because I believe you can actually do what I am suggesting. I have spoken a lot and written many books, and I have never been accused of being overly in-depth. Nope. I am a simple guy who needs easy, I-can-do-that–type ideas to move forward. If you are thinking, *Me too*, then this book is for you!

And here is a little math for you engineers reading this book: less suck = more hero.

You *can* become a better husband, and I really want to help you.

—Doug Fields
www.dougfields.com

INTRODUCTION

Any guy can fall in love—I did—and since you are reading this book, it is likely that you did too. Think about it—all it really takes to fall in love is having a pulse. And it only takes half a pulse to fall into lust . . . but you already knew that. Staying in love is another matter; staying in love requires a plan and some learned skills.

With a plan and some skills, you do not have to settle for "survive"; your marriage can *thrive*. The goal of your marriage was not simply to survive, right? You did not get married thinking that your relationship would not continue to thrive. I have performed a bunch of weddings, and no guy has ever pulled me aside and said, "I'm hoping to gut this thing out for a few years so I can walk away with the leather couch and minimal child support." No way! When you got married, your love was strong; your passion was intense; your dreams were big. Then somewhere along the way . . . something happened.

Contrary to *Men's Health* headline wisdom, love is not something that just happens to us. It may feel like that, but nothing could be further from the truth. There is an enemy of marriage who wants us to believe love is all about that adrenaline-rush feeling. That way, when the feeling fades (and it often will after about eighteen months or so) or we think we have lost it altogether, we are fertile ground for the unheroic seeds of our destruction—fantasizing about other women, rationalizing small choices (that often turn into big, sucky mistakes)—with the end result often being the destruction of our marriages.

Essential point: If you have already had one of those destructive relationships that blew up, I have some great news. It is in the past. It is over. Gone. Hopefully, you already have asked God for forgiveness, so it is forgiven. And if it is forgiven, it is really long gone. East-from-the-west gone. What you have is today. This moment. The next best step for you is to forget the past and not worry about the future (and certainly not worry about how the past will affect your future). You have today to start new and begin again. So do that.

For men this whole marriage thing is so much more difficult than we thought when we were dating and then engaged, right? Had we only known!

The dating relationship was explosive. Mysterious. Exciting. Everything was new. The way she walked was cute. Her laugh was contagious. You could stare at her for hours and just listen to her voice.

Then you married . . . and "fascinating" eventually morphed into "irritating." The way she walks is still cute but, now, with a tad more clothing. It is not her laugh that is contagious anymore but her cough, and so you keep your distance, throwing tissues at her when she asks for one, and you keep a gallon of hand sanitizer in your fanny pack. You have listened to her voice so often that you have built yourself a man cave just to be out of her vocal range.

Though many marriages, of course, are not this far gone, a high percentage are. What used to be delightfully refreshing is now painfully familiar. Now she is so, um, well, ordinary. The new has worn off. The *Wow!* has turned to *Oh no!* What once sizzled now barely manages a fizzle. What happened?

According to recent scientific research helping us better understand the dating and courtship years, here is what happened: Apparently there is an excitement and pleasure trigger in your brain that produces a drug called *dopamine*. It is like candy for your mind. It is quite confusing for us laypeople to comprehend, but basically, when you were dating, your brain began creating and dumping copious loads of dopamine throughout your brain, and *it felt great* every time you were with her! Some would say you were developing an addiction to love. So, technically, when you said, "I love you," you were actually stoned. Way to go—now you are a married *crackhead*!

But dopamine is not love. True love can produce dopamine, and this makes you feel good, but it isn't love. Love is a choice, and you need a plan, and you need to use skills to keep your marriage filled with love choices.

I realize that there are several different types of married men who will read this book. I obviously do not know what type of marriage you have, but it is likely your marriage might fit into one of the following categories:

1. **Strong marriage.** No marriage is perfect, but yours is doing well, and you are looking for ways to make it better. You jumped at the chance to read this book and figure out how to be more effective. Nice! Your wife bought you this book, and you actually thanked her and told her you look forward to reading it. Way to go!

2. **Average marriage.** Your marriage is okay, but you know it can be better (because it has been), and you want to move it from average to strong. I love that desire to change.

3. **Struggling marriage.** In some ways your marriage might be okay, but in other areas, you know that something isn't right. There are little snowballs of simmering anger and resentment, and they are rolling downhill, getting larger and more caustic day by day. She knows it too. Maybe that is why she bought you this book. My guess is that you did not thank her for this "gift."

4. **Circling-the-drain marriage.** Your marriage sucks. Both you and your wife have had enough. It feels as if the only pathway to peace and tranquillity is to go your separate ways. You are in trouble. But perhaps you have enough hope that something might change. Good . . . not good that it sucks but good that you have a little hope. Hang on to that hope as you continue through this book.

Whatever type of marriage you find yourself in today, I believe that you can improve it. In the following chapters I share with you seven very practical actions that I talk to guys about all the time, whether onstage in front of thousands or one-on-one while riding mountain bikes with a friend. I have seen firsthand what happens when men stop blaming their wives for everything and put these seven actions into play. They work! You make some changes, and your marriage will follow. We'll jump into the seven actions starting in chapter 3, but don't fall into the temptation to skip the first two chapters and jump straight into the "fix." If you do, you will miss what is really broken in your marriage as well as some great material on sex and why guys can't seem to get enough of it. Seriously. Do not skip chapter 1 or 2, or that will be like trying to put a Band-Aid on a hemorrhage. Don't be that guy. Take your time—there is too much at stake.

Speaking of time, improving your husband skills will take some time. But if you turn these seven actions into habits, either your wife is going to think you were abducted by aliens and your body was replaced with a pod version, or she will think something is wrong with you and you must be having an affair. I have had wives ask me, "What did you do with my husband?" I hope your wife will ask, "What has gotten into you? Who are you? Why are you so different? Who stole the little boy that was my husband and replaced him with a man? This dude is the hero I married." If this happens to you, man up and tell her the truth. You do not have to tell her that you used to suck (she knows), but tell her that you are trying to be less sucky now (by the way, that is very sexy to women . . . *trying*). I would love to be a fly on the wall for that conversation.

1

STOP CHASING THE WIND AND START CHASING YOUR WIFE

When I was little, like most boys, I wanted to be a super-hero. Specifically, I wanted to be Batman. He had cool gadgets and was a great fighter. When I became a hormone-filled preteen, I switched to wanting to be the Invisible Man . . . for obvious reasons.

As I grew out of my superhero phase, my dream evolved to becoming a professional athlete. Week after week I devoured *Sports Illustrated* with anticipation of what I wanted my life to look like. I was inspired by men breaking tackles, sinking three-pointers at the buzzer, hitting walk-off home runs with the crowds going wild, and I imagined myself achieving simi-lar greatness one day.

As I hit late adolescence, my athletic dream began to fade. I discovered that to become a professional athlete required that I actually had to be *good* at something. Even if I had been blessed with above-average athletic ability, I heard there was something involved in sports called *practice*. Just thinking about having to practice made me uncomfortable, triggering a love for Twinkies—which I became very proficient at consuming. So needless to say, I let go of that dream of being *SI*'s Athlete of the Year.

But the dream of greatness never left. I still wanted it though I was not sure what path to greatness I wanted to chase. When I got married, I thought I might pursue greatness in the bedroom, but after thirty-plus years of marriage, my wife, Cathy, still has not given me a trophy. But I haven't given up.

Men inherently possess a desire for greatness. I am guessing when you were a boy, you never said, "I'm going to strive for mediocrity with the hope of never achieving anything." Yet somewhere along the way your dreams for greatness crossed the intersection of reality, and life hit you broadside. It's not that you gave up the hope for greatness; it's just that *life* got in the way: responsibilities, pain, disappointment, careers, relationships that required work—or didn't work at all—unreasonable and unmet expectations, marriage, children, you name it.

Here's the sad truth: when our dreams fizzle, we simply learn to settle for lesser dreams. In fact, many of us settle for the crap that the culture has sold to us about what men are supposed to be like: we are supposed to chase *things*, and we took the bait, hook, line, and sinker.

For men it turns out that the object of the chase is not the important thing. In fact, it is secondary. We can chase prestigious careers, piles of money, positions with esteem, accolades from corporate headquarters, power to control others, women to conquer . . . whatever. It is the *act of chasing* that is important. But every man who has ever done the chase thing knows that even if we catch whatever it is we are chasing, the chase is never over. There is *always* something else to chase!

The sadder truth is it is never enough for men to chase after something. We want people (especially other men) to know that we have chased, captured, and won something along the way. This is why guys love trophies. It is interesting that an often-heard phrase is, "That's *his* trophy wife." You never hear, "That's *her* trophy husband." Why? Everyone knows women did not invent trophies. Guys did. Women invented other things—scrapbooking, Tupperware, and yeast infections—not trophies.

We are surrounded by this stereotypical, culturally correct man. He loves the chase, he works hard, he is strong, he has his pride, he conquers, he advances, he gets his way, he does what he wants, and when he drinks beer, he drinks Dos Equis.

Our culture paints the picture of a man's man who is driven by thoughts of, *I've got to close another deal. I've got to sign another contract. I've got to buy more property. I've got to re-fi another loan. I've got to land another bid. I've got to get ahead of him. I've got to get that promotion. I want what he has. I've got to say yes to more. I've got to say yes to the chase.*

It appears that a man's drive for the chase goes back thousands of years. The Old Testament book of Ecclesiastes was written by one of the most successful and prosperous men to ever live, the wisest of them all, King Solomon. Solomon appeared to have it all. In his forty-year reign over Israel, he spearheaded massive building projects, including the first temple in Jerusalem. He collected thousands of horses and chariots. He amassed great wealth and treasure. He was very much into the ladies, having seven hundred wives and three hundred concubines.

Seriously? He needed a thousand different women? I would hate to see his Visa bill after Hanukkah.

Solomon was a master of the chase. Yet, reflecting upon all he had accomplished, he wrote: "But as I looked at everything I had worked so hard to accomplish, it was all so meaningless—like chasing the wind" (Eccl. 2:11 NLT).

Sadly, we have bought into the cultural construct of manhood. We are addicted to the chase. We are busy, and our busyness validates our sense of importance. Yet we, like Solomon before us, are chasing the wind. We are too busy to notice that the chase is killing our souls, wounding our wives, and destroying our marriages.

Some of you reading these pages are having an affair. Maybe not with a woman, but with the chase. Your work is the object of your affection. Your phone is your mistress, and your laptop is your lover. The wind is getting your best efforts. When your wife carefully raises a caution flag about your busyness and lack of margin in life, you become defensive and blame her with a clever sentence like, "I've got to do all this so you can live the life that you want to live."

Really? Your wife may appreciate the lifestyle your chase can provide. But she likely would give it up in a heartbeat to have more of you in her life. She does not want your *presents*; she wants your *presence.*

Whenever I speak to women's groups, I hear them loud and clear that our chase is not their chase:

- "I'd rather have him make less money and be around more."
- "He's so engaged with work that he's not engaged at home."
- "I used to think he did this for the family, but in the end, it's more about his ego."

Guys, you are driven to provide for the needs of your family. This is the grain-of-truth, the God-given wiring, and the sacred cog of the chase. But many of us have managed to bury the truth under layers of self-interest and self-fulfillment until the truth has been lost. The point of the chase has become the chase itself.

I am not suggesting you shouldn't work hard, but I am suggesting that if you are defining your value by the chase—by your ambition, your work, and your achievement—then you are simply chasing after the wind, and ultimately, it is meaningless.

Busyness has become today's new status symbol. We treat it as a badge of honor. Conversations like this happen every day:

"Hey, how are you doing? Stayin' busy?"

"Oh, I'm slammed! You?"

"Yep, totally in over my head!"

"Yeah, me too. Can't believe the season we're in right now at work."

"I hear you. Who needs sleep?"

"Glad to hear you're doing well!"

"Yeah, you too. Congratulations!"

I'm sorry, but that type of interaction borders on insane! Now, I don't want to give the impression that I am never busy. In fact, struggling with busyness is an ongoing challenge for me. But I am no longer impressed with my own busyness or that of others.

What I have learned (in my own life and in my observation of others) is that busyness is usually a sign of brokenness.

So when a guy tells me about how busy he is, it is usually a sign that something is broken within—either relationally, emotionally, spiritually, or a combination of the three. Here is the point: there is a price to pay for busyness, and it is usually very expensive.

The busyness you experience in pursuit of the chase is an archenemy of being your woman's hero. The chase robs you of depth in your relationships, particularly your relationship with the most important human being in your life: your wife. When you are addicted to the chase, you have no time for building or maintaining depth in your marriage. You lose focus on what really matters, and the people you love become all too familiar. As Max Lucado, one of my favorite authors, wrote:

> He's an expert in robbing the sparkle and replacing it with the drab. . . . And his strategy is deceptive. . . .
>
> Nor will he steal your home from you; he'll do something far worse. He'll paint it with a familiar coat of drabness.
>
> He'll replace evening gowns with bathrobes, nights on the town with evenings in the recliner, and romance with

routine. He'll scatter the dust of yesterday over the wedding pictures in the hallway until they become a memory of another couple in another time. . . .

Hence, books will go unread, games will go unplayed, hearts will go unnurtured, and opportunities will go ignored. All because the poison of the ordinary has deadened your senses to the magic of the moment.[1]

The chase causes you to be overcommitted and underconnected. Something has to change, or your marriage will suffer the consequences.

Some years ago I performed a memorial service for a very wealthy man who died in his early fifties from the poison of busyness. It was a sad funeral. Everyone who spoke of the man talked about his work ethic, his vocational achievements (trophies), and his fortune. Clearly, he had been very successful in business. He owned multiple homes and had a lot of stuff that most people would consider the fruit of his labor. What I found tremendously sad was that he was a lousy husband and father. He was rarely home to enjoy his most valued possessions—his family.

Fast-forward a few years. I performed the wedding for this guy's widow when she remarried. Guess what? Her new husband is now enjoying the fruit of the dead guy's labor, which likely led to his fatal heart attack. I would like to ask the dead man, "How did all that chasing the wind work out for you?"

Here is the epilogue to this sad story: The man did not really want the toys. He wanted the chase. He died chasing the wind. The wife did not want all the toys. She wanted her husband. They both lost.

When we are addicted to the chase, we leave nothing to our wives but possessions and regrets. I will say it one more time, hoping that dawn will break over those with marble heads: Your wife doesn't want the presents your chase buys or the status your busyness conveys. She wants a vital and intimate relationship with you, and this requires your presence in her life. It requires you to make a proactive choice to invest your time and energy in your (one) life together.

And here is a bit of biblical truth to drive the nail home: There is only one thing on this earth the Bible talks about being one with. It's not your job, your kids, your ministry, your hobbies, your golf game, or your fantasy football team(s). It is your wife. And if you are chasing anything else at the expense of oneness with your wife, you are chasing the wind.

A hero is not created when a man chases the wind. A hero is created when a man recognizes he has been chasing the wrong things and realizes that his wife should be the object of his chase.

Husbands, remember the early days of romance with your wife? Remember when you chased after *her*, flirted with *her*, tried to win *her* attention, *her* thoughts, and *her* affection? Return to those days. Start chasing your wife again! Your relationship with her is far more meaningful than any money you will ever earn and far more important to your happiness than any work achievement you will ever attain.

Be her hero! Chase her. Don't stop chasing her. Ever. This

is a chase worthy of addiction. It is one that will pay off with a healthy, vibrant, and growing marriage.

In many ways this book is a "Chase Your Wife" manual. After the next chapter (which is about sex), I lay out proven principles for keeping your marriage constantly exciting. Yes, that means finding secrets to more and better sex. Without the glue of physical and emotional intimacy on a regular basis (yes, I said "emotional intimacy," and you'll soon discover why), no marriage has a chance. For sure, prayer, Bible reading, and serving together are fantastic and needed, but if they are not combined with the glue of intimacy, you may end up an *intact* couple, not an *intimate* one.

I know you . . . you don't want to settle for intact.

These seven secrets—that start in chapter 3—to becoming one with your wife, to not sucking as a husband, to being her hero in every way imaginable—are nearly everything I know about never settling for intact (and not letting *her* settle). While few men will be able to do all of them at once, over the course of several months or years, with God's help, a willing wife, and a little effort (okay, it will be one of the hardest challenges you have ever taken in your life), you will have what you signed up for when you said "I do."

Why? You finally will be doing what you said you would do when you said "I do" even though you had no idea you would actually need to do what needed doing. Got it?

Never mind. Let's get to chapter 2 and talk about sex.

2

How It Got Laid

Catchy chapter title, don't you think? Pardon my literary device, but I was hoping to grab your attention. It worked, right? You are such *a guy*.

But now that you have started this chapter, keep reading, as what follows is important. (And if you skipped the introduction and chapter 1, hoping to jump right into the good stuff, go back and read them now!)

The actions and skills I am challenging you to incorporate into your life come from a foundation that was laid long before you and I were gleams in our parents' eyes.

THE MARRIAGE INVENTION

Marriage did not evolve; it was God's invention. Sex was His idea! That's right; go ahead and say it with feeling. "Thank You, God!"

Perhaps you don't know a lot about God or the Bible. That's okay. But if you haven't heard this before, let me be the first to inform you that the Bible is not silent on sex, sexuality, or all-things-that-may-be-considered-sexy.

Want proof? Check out this Bible verse: "She is a loving deer, a graceful doe. Let her breasts satisfy you always. May you always be captivated by her love" (Prov. 5:19 NLT).

How awesome is that? I know some of you are thinking, *Dang, I never saw that verse in my Sunday school class.* I know! I can relate. My parents sheltered me from the best parts of the Bible too. Because of that deprivation I have collected a whole journal full of Bible verses like this one. I figured these verses were a great starting place to memorize Scripture for me and my buddies. *Let her breasts satisfy you always.* Golden. I bet you already have that verse memorized. I know most of my friends will read that sentence aloud to their wives. But sadly, Scripture wasn't given to us to use like a club to prove a point, so you really can't tape that one to your wife's pocket mirror and ask her to obey. Sorry.

Did you know that the Bible has an entire book filled with sexual imagery, called the Song of Songs? It is a book in which King Solomon vividly describes what he wants to do with his love—it appears she had a great personality. And from what I've read, she was pretty hot and wild.

The Sex Is . . . Well, Awesome!

I believe sex is one of the many proofs that there is a God. Sex was God's intelligent design.

If your mind hasn't already gone there, think about the female clitoris for a moment. Okay. That's long enough. If you don't know what it is (or know it by another name), it is part of the female genitalia. What is the purpose of the clitoris? This is not a trick question, and unfortunately there is not another Bible verse to memorize here. I want you to stop and consider the *why* of that little location on your wife's body. Its purpose is simply for pleasure. That's it! The clitoris plays no other biological function:

1. It doesn't help with urination.
2. It doesn't contribute to digestion.
3. And you can't use it to get better cable reception on your TV.

It is simply a female biological trigger for pleasure. Again, we pause to say, "Thank You, God. How wonderful is Your creation!"

It drives me crazy to think that evolution would get any credit for sex. Do you really think there could have been a caveman who *accidentally* discovered sex one day? Can you imagine Grog's hieroglyphic journal entry?

Grog run into tree. Ouch! Make face hurt. Then Grog run into Grogette. She soft. I like better. We fall down. I cheer her up. I call it sex.

In the first book of the Bible, we find the creation story, where God created this incredible playground we call Earth, and then He created man and woman. When He created man, "God said, 'It is not good for the man to be alone'" (Gen. 2:18 NLT).

At least on a superficial level, it seems as though Adam has it all. And if he does have it all, *isn't it all good?* There was no smog, no traffic, no crowds, no tension, no politics, no mother-in-law. What else could he possibly need—besides, of course, ESPN, UFC, and buffalo wings?

But God makes it clear that Adam did not have it all. He did not have all that was good because he was *alone*. We were created *not* to be alone. So then God created Eve, and Adam said, "At last! This one is bone from my bone, and flesh from my flesh!" (Gen. 2:23 NLT).

Adam's response sounds as if he is reading a user's manual for a first-aid kit . . . boring! Think about it, guys. Adam is the first man in the history of humanity to see a naked woman.

I may have too active of an imagination, but I can't imagine Adam waking up from his induced sleep, seeing a naked woman, and calmly saying, "At last, someone who can help me name the animals . . . and I hope she has a pleasant personality."

We know better. There is no way it happened like that. Men, can you imagine this scene? Actually, I know you can imagine and already have. Most men can quickly picture Eve naked in their minds right now. Stop it. Come back to this book.

Nevertheless, I am still betting that this was an extraordinary experience for Adam (talk about a dopamine rush!). He woke up from being put to sleep by God, and there was Eve—naked! Nude! Bare. Stripped. Undressed. Exposed. Uncovered. You get the idea. I wonder if that moment was also the genesis of the phrase "Praise God." *Praise God! Wrap her up! I'll take*

her. Better yet, let's not wrap her up. I'll take her just like that!
Could it be that Adam was the first man to sing (yell, scream),
"Come thou fount of every blessing"? Booyah!

You never know.

What we do know is God invented sex and marriage. It
was His idea. In Genesis 1, we read of the sixth day of God's
creation: "So God created human beings in his own image. In
the image of God he created them; male and female he created
them. . . . Then God looked over all he had made, and he saw
that it was very good!" (vv. 27, 31 NLT).

When God made men and women, including all of those
nifty parts that fit together so nicely and provide humans with
pleasure, He looked them over and called what He had made
"very good." When we read of all God created, it is fascinating
to note that men and women are the only parts of creation that
He says are *very good.* Everything else rated just *good.* Stars?
Good. Plants? *Good.* A Starbucks in every garden? *Good.* Lions,
tigers, and bears? *Good.* Humankind, male and female, marriage, and sex? *Very good.* This, to me, speaks volumes about
God's intention and the value He placed on the relationship
between man and woman.

MARRIAGE MATH: 1+1=1

After God created the first man and woman, we read the con-
clusion of the account in Genesis 2: "This explains why a man
leaves his father and mother and is joined to his wife, and the
two are united into one" (v. 24 NLT).

This passage shows God's goal for marriage: oneness. It points to the physical nature of the relationship (two united into one—come on; that is a fairly graphic representation of sexual intercourse). They were *joined* and *united* as one, and the emotional, spiritual, and sociological bonded (again, joined and united) into a family unit. Marriage is God's design, and His plan may sound like fuzzy math, but it is, nonetheless, true. God's goal for marriage is that 1+1=1.

Obviously you are free to believe whatever you want, but for thousands of years this has been the historical and biblical view of marriage. It is one man plus one woman making a monogamous commitment to be united as one.

In the New Testament, Jesus confirms this definition of marriage and adds an exclamation point:

> "Haven't you read the Scriptures?" Jesus replied. "They record that from the beginning 'God made them male and female.'" And he said, "'This explains why a man leaves his father and mother and is joined to his wife, and the two are united into one.' Since they are no longer two but one, let no one split apart what God has joined together." (Matt. 19:4–6 NLT)

ONE HEART

Marriage isn't simply about creating physical oneness. The truth is, we don't have to create it. When two people marry, they become one. We just have to figure out how to live out marriage as one, united so that no one will split us apart.

Here is a perspective that became a game-changer in my own marriage. It literally transformed my outlook, which in turn reformed my knuckleheaded actions to be a lot less "knuckleheadish." The perspective is what I have come to call the *One Heart Principle*. Are you ready for it? Really? I promise it can change everything in your marriage. If you're ready, hang on to your pancreas and open your heart. It is this: in marriage, when I wound or hurt or trample on my wife's heart, I am really doing the same to my own heart. Or the more positive way to look at it is this: when I *enhance* my spouse's heart, I am really *enhancing* my own at the same time.

This is a no-brainer. It is almost too simple to be true. If, by God's design, my wife and I are one, then when I hurt my wife, I hurt myself too. On the other hand, when I build up her heart, I also build up myself. That is the powerful dynamic of oneness.

Think about it. The subtle or not-so-subtle verbal shots you take at your wife may make sense in your head in the heat of the moment, but they are *not* damage free. They might appear innocent. They might even be part of the how-we-relate-to-each-other script that has played itself out over the years. But they are *not* innocent, and they always result in damage—to her and to yourself.

I am glad my memory can't count how many times I have said something that I knew was going to hurt Cathy. Being totally naive about the One Heart Principle, I always thought *she* was the target. When I am mad, hurt, wounded, ticked, frustrated, peeved, no problem: take those feelings, mold them into words, and fire them from the cannon of my mouth at the intended target (aka *spouse*). I can't believe how stupid I was! She wasn't the target of my hurtful words; *we* were the target. You know what I'm referring to. In a sucky moment you say something that could sound funny but would also send a message that you want to get across (e.g., "If you eat another piece of that pie tonight, you'll be wearing it in the morning." On the funny scale it's about a 2 out of 10. On the jerk scale it rates a lot higher.) Anger can turn your spouse into an easy target. Whenever a buddy of mine wanted to make a point that his wife was trying to emasculate him by doing or saying something that obviously was meant to bring him down a notch as a man, he used to call her by the name of his mother-in-law (who everyone knew was over-controlling and insensitive). "It felt good for about five seconds," he said. "Then I could see the hurt in her eyes, and I realized I'd just wounded two hearts with one cheap shot."

In your marriage you have One Heart, and when you wound your spouse, you wound yourself too. Imagine shooting a gun that has a curved barrel pointing back at your heart. I don't know anyone who would willingly shoot that gun. But that's really what's happening to our relationships when we hurt our wives. As (biblically) one, we hurt ourselves.

The One Heart Principle means that as a husband who wants to be healthy and happy and experience the same qualities in marriage, I must be vigilant to protect our One Heart in whatever I say and do.

In a much broader context Jesus shared a similar thought in how we relate to others: "Do to others whatever you would like them to do to you. This is the essence of all that is taught in the law and the prophets" (Matt. 7:12 NLT).

You have probably heard this passage referred to as the *golden rule*. In this verse Jesus says that the entirety of the Scriptures' teaching can be summed up in treating others the way you want to be treated. Now, if Jesus said this was the standard for how we should treat *everyone*, how much more should we apply this standard to our own *wives*, with whom we are united *as one*?

But wait; there's more! In the New Testament book of Ephesians, we find the essence of the One Heart Principle (we will talk a bit more about this later on). In Ephesians 5:28–29, we read: "In the same way, husbands ought to love their wives as they love their *own* bodies. For a man who loves his wife actually shows love for *himself.* No one hates his *own* body but feeds and cares for it, just as Christ cares for the church" (NLT, emphasis added).

When you grasp this One Heart Principle, it can radically revolutionize your marriage. I realize that there can be a lot of pain in marriage, but I would venture to say that most spouses, at their core, really do not want to hurt each other. In my own marriage I don't want Cathy to hurt me. So why would I ever want to hurt her? Also, I am fully confident that I would never intentionally hurt myself. Don't miss this, guys! Because you are one with your wife, why would you want to hurt your wife *and* yourself? If you embrace the One

Heart Principle, it will profoundly change the trajectory of your marriage.

Having One Heart at the forefront of your brain does not mean you will do it right all the time. Pursuing the One Heart Principle is all about motive, not perfection. A good friend of mine is married to a woman with some very significant PTSD (post-traumatic stress disorder) issues. He told me, "I accidently hurt her by something I say at least once a month. Sometimes she takes it personally because the abuse she faced in a previous marriage was so bad. Other times she realizes I'm a guy and can't help myself. My job as a guy is to make mistakes, and I'm very good at it." But then he taught me a "get out of jail" phrase I am starting to incorporate into my own male relational tool chest: "I am so sorry that I hurt you. I know I'll make many more mistakes as time goes on, but I'll try not to make *that one* again."

Your wife can learn to tolerate your male, um, idiosyncrasies, as long as your intent is never to hurt but always to strengthen and build up—to treat her heart as if it were your own . . . because it is.

So where are we headed together? Though I write and speak, I am a pretty normal male who is trying to follow in the ways of Jesus. Keeping it simple in this book was pretty easy.

This little formula will make it even simpler: one man chasing his wife (chapter 1) + a firm belief in One Heart in marriage (chapter 2) + these seven important actions (chapters 3–9) = a healthy and growing marriage for years to come.

──────2B──────

The Flip Side

N ow that you have finished chapter 2, you flip the page and see *another* chapter 2. What's that about? Well, men like getting bonuses, and this chapter is really the "cut you a break" addition to the chapter you just read. Not *every* marriage problem is a man's fault. That is why I have written a response, a B chapter to follow most of the chapters in this book. These shorter B chapters are designed to answer the questions,

"What if it's really not my fault in this particular area? What if my wife is more the one with the issue than me?"

Well, I get it. That happens sometimes. So in these bonus chapters, I have addressed what to do if your wife may be more of the problem in this category than you. But my guess is, about 85 percent of the time, it won't be applicable.

──────

While it doesn't happen often, there are relationships where the male is the more sensitive one in the relationship. For whatever reason, the wife can be mean as nails, cold as ice, and perhaps a dozen other clichés. Her biting comments or attempts at sarcastic humor both make you feel like crap and make you feel less of a man.

And when it comes to the intimacy factor, she doles it out only on birthdays or when you've hit husband perfection for thirty days in a row. (Good luck with that streak.)

No matter what your foundation and beliefs about one-ness in marriage, there are circumstances that will test that foundation to the core. Most marriages start out strong; both spouses are on their best behavior. But then life hits, perhaps a kid or two or three, and all of a sudden, the woman who used to be so nice and passionate is doing everything she can (it seems) to deny your deepest needs.

Every marriage goes through seasons where the ebb and flow of passion ebbs a bit longer than you think you can take. How do you stay One Heart with her when you want a normal sex life and she doesn't? What do you do when she is meaner than you expected any woman could be to your sensitive heart?

And what happens when she doesn't have this same One Heart perspective as you do? While you are trying to be her hero and have this unselfish One Heart thing appearing more often, you are going to need some help along the way. We need our women to give us some encouragement. But if they don't, one thing we don't do is abandon our pure motive of being One Heart with her.

Heroes do not abandon doing the heroic thing because they don't get their way.

They persevere.

A huge percentage of women will come around if they see a man's consistency, patience, forbearance, and long-suffering . . . his unconditional love. It will be a very rare woman who won't.

Truth: Heroes stay heroes when they don't get the immediate results they hope for (more and better sex). They don't malfunction in the dark if they don't get their way in the light. That's what a fly-by-night hero does, not a true hero who cares for his woman's heart and cares that the One Heart in marriage is really One Heart.

ONENESS KILLERS

Blame and competition are the two areas men struggle with that compete against oneness. And if your wife is a bit mean— or even ignores you more than you like—the blame comes easier.

The truth is, men and women (especially with kids in the home) compete for personal-space time (me time), and then blame the other when they don't get it because their tanks are depleted to the point of not being able to give to the other. Men, this is when the One Heart marriage leans into each other, not to blame or compete but to work equally until the work is done. Being her hero means seeking to fill her tank, seeking to help her avoid those things that deplete her tank so that your *combined* tank gets full together.

Back to blame. Because we guys are typically a bit more selfish than women, we are quick to point blame at anyone but ourselves. Blame comes quickly and creatively to the male mind. We can blame cats and dogs and inanimate objects and in-laws and parents and especially our wives. Blame can be traced all the way back to Adam taking a shot at Eve: "It was the woman *you gave me* who gave me the fruit" (Gen. 3:12 NLT, emphasis added). Yes, we have been blaming the woman for a few millennia. For me, I am fairly good at finding blame when my three basic needs aren't met: sex, sleep, and food (sometimes in that order). So when I'm forgetting to do the little things that fill her tank (yes, forgetting *is* a main theme for some of us men), such as

- emptying the trash,
- fixing the leak in the sink,
- putting my clothes in one of the two (yes, two) laundry baskets in our bedroom, or
- keeping my agreement to hang out with the kids so she could have a girls' night out (instead, I booked a poker game at our house),

she sometimes will forget my needs.

The reason we like to blame? We don't want to look bad. We are also a bit too competitive and don't want to lose. We are prideful dolts who can barely spell *humility*, let alone be humble.

On the plus side, this attitude serves us well in war, sports, and our businesses (sometimes). It keeps us striving, trying to win, and that ultimately helps feed our families, protect freedom, and win trophies that collect dust in our man caves.

So if you are playing the blame game in your competitive drive to be the man and win every argument and not look bad, how is that working for you? No need to answer; I already know.

FROM WHENCE SHE CAME

All women are radically different.

They come to the marriage with mom baggage, dad baggage, hormone and/or brain baggage, junior high baggage, old boyfriend baggage, and sometimes sexual abuse baggage (a full one-third of women fall into this sad category), not to mention girls' and women's magazines baggage that have all but destroyed their ability to feel good about themselves as God made them to be. We will hit on more of this later, but you must know that there are reasons why she sometimes acts the way she does toward you.

Your biggest, most important job as the hero husband of her life is to identify the baggage, help her unload it, and then fill it up with what God would want her to know—how precious and wonderful she truly is. It is not an impossible job but a job that humble heroes welcome, embrace, and actively try to complete. We are doers and fixers, and though no one (including you) wants to be fixed, we sorta *all* need good and loving fixing.

So if your spouse has way more baggage than most (you probably really don't, but if it makes you feel better about your daily challenges, I'll let you believe you do), cut the blame game and competitive *ta-da-ta*, drop the pride, and do the work needed to fill her tank and keep it full.

And *not* so you can have more sex.

(Weak. Motive. Men.)

Do it because she is the other half of your heart, and you need that half of your heart filled to the brim with health and happiness. And while this isn't your motive for filling her heart, the truth is you need her full so that when you've hit a half-full season in your own life, she is there to help fill in your low spots. You may not have them now, but you will. And that is why it is not good for man to be alone. We have *lots* of low spots in our lives, and a woman usually knows how to fill them.

Truth: heroes look at the long view of oneness and keep their eyes on that horizon. When they do, they get a true marriage.

So as we now move into the seven practical actions of becoming a better husband, never forget these foundations:

1. Marriage is God's design and His idea.
2. Marriage is God's plan for you to be a hero and for her to be there for you when you need her.
3. Experiencing oneness with your wife is God's goal for your marriage.

When you base your marriage on this foundation, you will be more willing to fight, to work, to strive . . . to not suck at your marriage. Without this as your foundation, all of the actions I am about to suggest to improve your marriage may be *nice*, but essentially they will be powerless.

3

ACTION #1:
DON'T SAY EVERYTHING YOU THINK

I have a buddy whose wife walked into the family room as he was watching TV and simply asked, "How do you like my new haircut?"

He turned her way, scanned her new coif, and confidently replied, "It looks nice. Sorta like you're back in high school."

She replied, "Hmmm. I'll give you a do-over! Why don't you try that one again—how do you like my new haircut I spent $150 on?"

He said, "I'm trying to tell you it looks great. I'm not sure it's $150 worth of great though."

My friend slept on the couch that night.

The first action that will help you improve as a husband is extremely simple and logical to understand, but it is quite difficult to put into practice in marriage:

DON'T SAY EVERYTHING YOU THINK.

I promise—you don't have to. I realize this call to action may disorient the male brain. I know you think you have to say everything that comes into your mind, but you don't. Really! If you can learn to master this, you will become heroic. Although it is a lot easier said than done.

My own personal struggle with not saying everything I think revolves around three primary issues: (1) I have a quick wit, (2) I have a bent toward sarcasm, and (3) I have an under-developed, weak self-control fiber running from my brain to my mouth. Any one of these issues can be problematic in marriage, but combined together they become a dangerous and toxic mixture.

A good starting point for most guys is to make a simple admission that mastering this action is going to be difficult . . . make that *very difficult*. Go ahead and confess it right now. If you don't want to say it aloud because you are reading this on a plane or in a crowded Taco Bell, I understand, but at least admit—to yourself, silently—how tough this is going to be. Making hurtful and mean-spirited comments is too easy, especially when you are, like me at times, simply stupid. How smart was I several years ago when I was pondering whether to tell my pregnant wife, "Honey, it looks like you've picked up some weight over the holidays"? And, truth be told, how smart can it be to even be having a serious internal dialogue with yourself that is even asking this question? See, I'm not always so intelligent.

But the challenge doesn't stop at just being stupid. To avoid saying what pops into your mind becomes even more difficult when you are defensive, angry, or tired with low blood sugar—or any combination of the three.

For me, being tired is a real killer. Fatigue has a history of leading me to make more bad decisions and more hurtful or dumb comments than any other challenge I face.

Not long ago Cathy made a simple request: "Will you please grab your McDonald's cup you left in my car so it doesn't break through the bottom and leak all over the place?"

Her reason for making the request was a sound one. The "cup explosion" has happened before. And just like asking a nonpregnant woman when is she due, I wish I could say I had done that only once. Numerous times, I have left my half-full paper cup of Diet Coke in the car, and those nutritious chemicals ate through the paper and blew out the bottom of the cup, naturally leaving a sticky mess—and a ticked-off wife.

So her preventive ask was really a fair request. But the problem was that I was tired (which, as I mentioned above, makes me more vulnerable to think and say stupid things). It had been a long and tough day at work, and I didn't want to walk *all the way* from the couch out to the driveway (approximately twenty-seven yards away). Honestly, I wondered why she didn't just bring in the cup herself. I wanted to say (again, see my comments on tired and stupid above), *"How hard would it have been for you to bring the cup in? Is it filled with lead? Dynamite, perhaps? Rat droppings?! Come on! It's not like I'm sitting around being a slacker. I'm working hard all day to pay for a car that has some really nice special features—like a cup holder!"*

That is what I wanted to say, but while I may be stupid, I'm not that stupid. Fortunately I didn't.

Unfortunately, I didn't keep my mouth shut either (see previous comment about my issue of weak self-control). I snapped off a terse, "Couldn't you have just brought it in?" In doing so, I immediately catapulted myself from hero to fool. I bet you have your own stories, don't you?

This is not a new problem; stupid-talk has been around for a long time. Here is some straightforward wisdom from the Old Testament book of Proverbs: "Even fools are thought wise when they keep silent; with their mouths shut, they seem intelligent" (17:28 NLT). "Too much talk leads to sin. Be sensible and keep your mouth shut" (10:19 NLT).

Way to go, Doug! On this occasion I wasn't even able to raise my rank to silent fool.

Yet even if I had managed not to say anything, I likely still would have blown it. My facial expression at Cathy's request would have dramatically revealed what I was thinking. As you know, *nonverbal* communication is often more powerful than words. Many of us guys have perfected the art of the eye roll in response to our wives' requests. We have convinced ourselves that a head shake, a smirk, an eye roll is better than saying something harsh or hurtful. The truth is, our nonverbal responses can wound our spouses *just as much* as a biting comment.

Pay attention here: Not saying everything you think isn't about choosing to allow your body language to do the talking instead of speaking your thoughts aloud. *It's about refraining from both!* Keeping quiet and still. Guys, we might be slow to understand this, but make no mistake about it: both our words *and* our body language *are always communicating something* to our wives. Nonverbal is equally as strong as verbal.

In my house our kitchen counter can become pretty cluttered. It is a collecting station for family stuff: mail, unpaid bills, our kids' backpacks, coupons I am sure I will use someday, and half-full cups of Diet Coke. Sometimes when my outer world is out of control, I want my home to be clean so I can at least have an illusion of control in some area of my life. I realize clutter at home doesn't bother a lot of guys, but it bugs me. You might think I have issues, and of course I do. But I'm working on them.

Okay, so I get a little annoyed by mess even though I have been working really hard over the last decade to get to the point of "Who cares?" Really, in the grand scheme of things, who cares if the kitchen counter is clean? There will be a day very soon when we don't have children in our house, and it will be both clean *and* quiet. But until then, who cares? The kitchen counter is messy. Some of this is my fault. Some of it is my kids' fault. And some of it is my wife's fault. (And, yes, I'm too smart to assign percentages of fault and share them with you.)

There is a portion of the counter where I prepare a little post-workout protein shake. If you ever saw me in person, you might be tempted to think my muscles were all natural. But as difficult as it is for me to admit, I've had help. (It's also difficult to admit I don't really have muscles, but since this isn't a picture book, I'll let you imagine a really good-looking, muscular author.) I have actually purchased my physique with cases of protein powder. Apparently, when I make my protein shake, I have been known to leave a little bit of powder on the counter. The key word to remember in this story is *little*.

It seems that just as the hungry falcon can spot a field mouse from a mile in the air, my wife has superhuman vision capable of seeing a *little* chocolate powder on a dark counter. I never notice it because I possess only normal human vision. Cathy, on the other hand, could be called in to a CSI unit to check for trace amounts of powder. I don't know how it happens, but the point is that she does notice.

So one day the falcon Cathy swooped in and said to me very calmly and matter-of-factly, "It seems like I'm always cleaning up powder after you." And I, the field mouse, went into survival mode. As if on cue, *Boom!* My mind scurried to safety—to the triangulation of (1) quick wit, (2) sarcasm, and (3) weak self-control.

My brain immediately conjured up this gem: *Oh, don't worry about cleaning the powder that only scientists can see. Instead, oh, I don't know . . . why don't you clean your* piles *that are big enough to have their own ecosystems? In fact, I think a family of armadillos has moved in between several of the largest ones. I hear* they *like protein powder. Just blow it into the rest of* your *mess, and they can have a nutritious dinner.*

Yes, that's what I conjured up. Good one, huh? I'm kind of proud of it. I didn't even have to think that hard: it immediately came to my mind. You may be a fast wordsmith too. Some of us guys can't speak in complete sentences when our wives want us to talk to them, but when we are defensive, we can conjure up articulate sentences at the speed of light. Fortunately, I didn't say it.

Here's what I did:

- I did not say what I thought—even though I was *so* tempted.
- I received Cathy's comment and thought that now would be a good time to not suck as a husband.
- I very respectfully said, "Oh, I'm sorry. I don't want you to have to clean up after me. I will definitely be more careful."

I know what some of you are thinking. You are thinking that just like when jumping into a mountain spring–fed lake, my manhood shriveled up and retracted to the nether regions when I made that statement to my wife. But actually, it's just the opposite. After more than thirty years of marriage, I have learned that my manhood is a lot happier when I treat my wife with respect and honor. You see, we become more heroic men when we treat our wives with the honor they really do deserve.

We treat our wives with honor when we don't say everything we think but instead seek to promote peace with our wives rather than enhance conflict. Here is another gem from the book of Proverbs: "It is to one's honor to avoid strife, but every fool is quick to quarrel" (20:3).

At least in this particular situation, I made the right choice and rose above fool status.

You can make the right choices too. I know you can. Let me say it again: holding your tongue and keeping your body language in check is not easy. In fact, it is almost always hard when you feel that you need to say something. Obviously, there are circumstances when you must speak up, but *what* you say and *how* you say it can make a world of difference, for better or for worse.

Snark-Infested Waters

A buddy of mine lives in what I refer to as *child hell*. This means he has five kids under the age of ten.

All boys!

Just watching this guy and his wife trying to navigate car seats, shoes, Cheetos-stained hands, and kids kicking each other is an absolute comedy show.

Cathy and I once pulled up next to them in the church parking lot as they were getting out of their minivan. I stood in amazement and awe, watching all that has to happen to prepare them to go into the public. It was like watching five crazed velociraptors running amok in a parking lot.

As a husband, when you find yourself thick in the weeds of real life, family, and marriage, moments like these are frustrating. You can feel the anger bubbling up inside you like gas after a chili lunch, and it doesn't take much motivation to let one fly. For my buddy, all it took was his wife innocently but exhaustedly saying, right there in the parking lot, "I wish we had more time."

This was a simple statement of fact. It was a neutral comment. She wasn't attacking; she was releasing frustration: *I wish we had more time.* Sure! Who doesn't? That is an understandable statement. If I were her, I might have said I wished I were in Iraq.

My buddy, who was also frustrated by his attempts to round up his kids (a feat not unlike trying to herd five cats hopped up on crack-laced catnip), immediately said, "I seem to remember *one* of us wanting to leave the house earlier." It's almost impossible to read his comment without throwing in a little "I can identify with that comment."

Okay, on the surface, that doesn't seem like a terrible remark, right? It is the type of comment that is pretty easy for us guys to make. (It *was* true, after all!) But if we look a little closer, the comment was snarky and demeaning. Let's pause and consider what happens when we direct unnecessary remarks at our wives:

1. **It creates defensiveness.** "I seem to remember *one* of us . . ." Clearly, my buddy did not mean his wife, so in saying this he was, in fact, attacking her by claiming superiority. Normally when attacked, people become defensive. Fool status is so easy to reach.

2. **It stirs anger.** In this illustration, it is highly likely that what she heard him say was, "You want more time? Puh-lease. I told you we needed to start getting ready earlier. You ignored me. This is your fault, and now I have to live with the consequences of your poor decisions. This happens all the time. I wish you were

a better mom, wife, and human." Even though that is not what he said, in the midst of anger, spouses can hear the reoccurring messages that have been deposited into their typical relating-scripts. She is mad that he is mad. Anger is being stirred. He is getting angry because of his wife's poor planning, and she is getting angry because she is being blamed. Her mind races to the fact that he wasn't even at home to help—he was out exercising while she was scurrying to pack diaper bags, snacks, and Prozac.

3. **It communicates a lack of respect.** Was there really a need for my buddy to point out his wife's flaw? Was this the time to do it? No and no. There may well be a need for a couple to discuss clock management, but this wasn't the moment for a decent conversation. Letting the snarky comment fly was disrespectful, and the message was both sent and received.

4. **It induces shame.** At times I suck, and at times you suck. It's a given. Ownership of sucking doesn't rest in men only (although we are the majority shareholders). No one is perfect. Everyone sucks at times. Do we need our wives to point out our flaws? No. We already know them well enough. So why in the world would we think that turning a spotlight on our wives' imperfections is a good idea? Simple answer: *It's not!* Pointing out our spouses' flaws only serves up a dish of shame.

5. **It adds credibility to any negative feelings she has of you.** You can be sure that your wife is aware of your

flaws. When we make unnecessary and demeaning remarks, we actually highlight and punctuate our own flaws for our wives, who may legitimately reply, "That's so typical of you!" Ouch.

The bottom line is that when you make a snarky comment to your wife, you don't win! You wound your wife, and you wound yourself (remember the One Heart Principle), so you lose, and you bring grief into your marriage. Your marriage doesn't need more grief. You can help reduce the grief quotient substantially by not saying everything you think. Follow the advice from Proverbs 21:23: "Watch your words and hold your tongue; you'll save yourself a lot of grief" (MSG).

BUT WHAT ABOUT HER
KNOWING SHE'S WRONG?

Yes, there are circumstances in marriage when something needs to be said. Some husbands seem to go to great lengths to avoid saying anything, even when it is necessary. Sure, these guys feel tension, but they just internalize it. As their anxiety builds to a boil, they grow ulcers, have heart attacks, or become chronic masturbators. Quite frankly, silence does not help your marriage, and in fact, it may threaten your life or at least give you an inappropriately powerful handshake.

The key to not sucking as a husband is not found in keeping silent. Rather, you can become a better husband simply by not saying everything you think and by thinking about what you say before you say it.

Let's go back to the story of my buddy who has the five Tasmanian devils (aka *active boys*). Let's recall the comment to his wife: "I seem to remember *one* of us wanting to leave the house earlier."

Let's consider his options at that moment in the parking lot:

- He can be a fool and make the snarky comment, ticking off his wife, who is now mulling over his comment the entire afternoon;
- or he can be her hero by saving the hurtful comment, loving her in the midst of her frustration, and thinking through the deeper principle—the issue that really needs to be addressed—and then making an appropriate and constructive comment at a later time.

In this instance the deeper principle is family time management and how to work together to get the pack of wild monkeys ready to be on time for a family event.

This may well be a perfectly valid point and brings up an issue that needs to be discussed with his wife. Great! In families with young kids, time management is likely a frequent topic. I have three women in my family, and I have learned that being "dressed" is not the same thing as being "ready to go." Typically for my son and me, when we are dressed, we are ready to go. Not so with women. For them, there is this whole face-as-a-construction-project thing that includes spackling, taping, and painting. Let me put this in terms that can be understood by guys: when a female says, "I'll be ready in five minutes," it's like you saying, "I'm just going to play one more game."

In this case the heroic comment from my buddy to his wife would have been, "Hey, when we have some time, let's put our heads together and see if we can figure out a better way to help each other get ready when we try to leave the house. I want to be better at this."

In our years of marriage, Cathy and I have figured out a way to deal with family issues that makes it easier for us to avoid mistimed, inappropriate, snarky remarks. We learned that having a weekly meeting to discuss our family business and relationship issues is a huge help. I am well aware that my choice of words (*weekly meeting*) might evoke some resistance from your wife. I get it! At first Cathy wasn't doing backflips and asking me about my favorite lingerie on her. Seriously, the idea of "a meeting with my husband" didn't trigger her romance meter. She would say that it even smacked of being a little condescending. If your wife doesn't get excited about scheduling a meeting, minimize the word *meeting* and suggest that you need a specific time each week when you can talk to her about what matters. (That will get her.)

For us, this weekly connection is where we bring together our agendas and talk calendar, responsibilities, finances, kids, and what may be bugging us, as well as what's working in our marriage. What began as a let's-get-on-the-same-page meeting often turns into a time of affirmation, where I pour it on about what I love about her. What all began as an experiment (by the way: use that word—*experiment*—with your wife because if the experiment doesn't work, no big deal—ditch it; it was just an experiment) has turned into one of the highlights of our week. It is never really a highly emotionally charged time because we have had *time* and *space* to think about what needs to be addressed before our meeting. There have been times when I have saved a minor conflict (by not saying anything when it happened) and thought, *I'll just bring this up when we meet on Monday.* Sometimes I have even forgotten what bothered me earlier in the week. And if I do recall something big enough to mention, I typically bring it up by using the "sandwich method" of confrontation.

This is so easy even a guy like me can understand. The bread of the sandwich is positive, upbeat, caring, and affirming. The meat of the sandwich is the difficult part of the conversation. I start with some highlights from the week and what I noticed about her but didn't have the opportunity to say. This is where I want to genuinely reveal something from my heart that lets her know how important and special she is to me. For example: "When I went mountain bike riding with the guys last week, I was listening to some of them complain, and I couldn't help but think how blessed I am to have married you. I watch in amazement at the way you help our kids navigate life. You're an incredible mom, and I'm so lucky to be with you for life."

You have just affirmed her in a genuine way. Key word: *genuine.* You have now won the right to be heard when and if you need to say anything tough (the meat of the sandwich):

"I'm not sure you were even aware of it, but the other day when Cassie came home frustrated at her best friend, I could tell you were distracted with making dinner. It didn't appear like you were really listening to her when you said, 'You need to get over it. You've done the same thing to her.' I saw the look in her eye, and she appeared to be pretty hurt."

Then you end with another positive comment: "Babe, you're normally so attentive and caring that I knew you must have had other things on your mind. So if your heart leads, you may want to bring up the episode with her to hear what she thought. It's not a huge deal, but I thought you'd want to know what I saw."

If you have heard this method before and you are not using it, then this will be a reminder. Almost anyone can handle what you really need to say if it is carefully communicated with sincere love and affirmation. And timing. Unless someone's life is in danger, rarely do you have to confront an issue the moment it happens. (I wish young parents would heed this same advice in the McDonald's Playland.) Wait until everyone is calmed down, you are having a good day, and you can look back with perspective about how big of a mountain you really want to make of something that simply may be a molehill. Then sandwich your comments with other truths from the heart.

To truly be her hero, you don't say everything you think when you think it.

Give it a try! You might not hit 100 percent right away, but that's okay. When you slip up, you'll probably quickly recognize it. That's a step in the right direction. Keep practicing.

One last piece of advice: when you experience a personal victory by keeping your mouth shut, don't celebrate that reality with your wife. "I was going to say this to you . . . but I didn't. I'm so proud of myself." Don't say that because, well, that would suck, and you would return to fool status.

———————3B———————

THE QUEEN OF SNARK...
NOW WHAT?

S ometimes it is not the man who is the snarkiest; it's the
woman. What happens if you are married to Her Highness
of Snark and Sarcasm? What if she is busting your chops every
chance she gets—deserved and undeserved? What if she gets
defensive nearly every time you bring something up, even
when you do it nicely, and then turns it around to an attack
on you? What if her ill-timed words cut you to the quick and
embarrass you in front of others?

If you are a follower of Jesus, you are likely aware that
Ephesians 5:25 instructs us to love our wives as Christ loved
the church. Yes, we die for our wives, but it doesn't mean we sit
idly by and take abuse, good-natured or not. It challenges our
feelings of being a man, sets a poor example for any daughter
wondering how to treat her man in the future, and oftentimes,
if done in public, is more embarrassing for her than it is for
you. The passages in the Bible that talk about holding your

tongue, and kindness, and speech filled with grace are legion. So if her words are cutting your heart out or are just plain mean, you cannot let it continue.

So what does it really look like to lay down our lives for the other halves of our hearts when they are hurting or shaming our half?

1. **Understand where it often comes from.** Snarkiness is a survival method people use to make them feel better about themselves. It is often learned deeply in childhood, usually because a parent was so hurtful or dismissing, they had to do *something* to make themselves not feel so bad. So if they could give it back without facing a backhand, it was likely an effective way not to be so weighed down with shame. It put the spotlight on the parent or other adult and *his or her* faults instead of any minor or major mistake they made. It truly is the sign of a deeper issue that hasn't been dealt with.

2. **Realize its impact.** Making humorous and appropriate comments is great. And sometimes, when you are in the right company and it is not mean-spirited, a little snark can be fine. But a constant barrage of snark and sarcasm can wear you down. And I'm not even talking about being plain mean. You have to honestly talk with your wife about how it makes you feel when it is done in the wrong way at the wrong time. This is one issue you have to nip in the bud, or your heart for her and your marriage will eventually close off. Snarky people are usually

also more defensive, so you have to make sure the time is right.

3. **Don't expect change overnight; give lots of grace.** Habits are hard to break, and if the rut of snark in your home is deep, it will take time to find a new trail or fill in the rut. Let it. Hopefully you haven't allowed it to go on for so long that you need an immediate and 180-degree change in a week. When it happens at a bad time, often a look is all you need to give her. Perhaps a couple days later it can be discussed. She may feel as though she is walking on eggshells so as not to do something to hurt "your tender feelings." If she uses a line like that, you have to nip *that* one in the bud too. She is using defensiveness so she doesn't have to change. She needs to change. Help her. Be her hero.

And this is another perfect spot to try the sandwich method:

"You do so much to make our home a house of grace and peace. I love how you pray for our family and take care of us in so many ways.

"But your sarcasm and snarkiness have embarrassed me and hurt me more than once. I'm not trying to be a softy here, nor do I want to attack your character. We just have to find a way to temper your comments more often. It's really doing a number on our heart as a couple.

"We do so many great things as a couple and a family,

and I know that will continue. We help others, point our kids to Jesus . . . lots of great things."

Being her hero means protecting both your hearts so that your One Heart will strengthen through the years. That means honest and swift and kind communication until the hurtful words are a thing of the past. And this leads perfectly into the next key point for being her hero: using your words in uplifting and powerful ways.

4

ACTION #2:
SAY WHAT IS POWERFUL

One of the greatest mistakes husbands make in marriage is that we say the things we should not say and don't speak words that are powerful, inspirational, and life-giving to our wives.

The marriage relationship is built or destroyed by words. Let me oversimplify this deep concept:

- Bad marriages are full of destructive words.
- Good marriages are full of powerful and inspirational words.

The problem with a lot of us thickheaded husbands is that we think our words are *inspirational* when, in fact, they are *destructive*.

> **HUSBAND:** "Sweetie, you would look so great if you could fit into that dress!"
>
> **WIFE:** "You're a jerk!"

HUSBAND: "What? I was just saying how good you'd look! Geez, I try to give you a compliment, and you get offended. Nice."

The wife was offended because the remark *was* offensive. She was right! The husband *was* a jerk. Let's be honest; his comment was an attempt to manipulate her into losing a few pounds. What a dweeb. Words of manipulation not only damage your own heart (remember the One Heart Principle), but they never work in the long term. Rather, words of manipulation tear down. Your wife is *not* going to be motivated by negative remarks. So no matter how well you think those negative comments from your dad or coach helped you perform better when you were a child, speaking that way *doesn't* work between you and the other half of your heart. You are not a hero if you can shame her into temporary change.

What's the antidote? Using words that actually have the ability to bring about real and lasting change. You can use words that are actually powerful.

These words are also known as encouragement and affirmation. They are words that inspire your wife, your teammate, the other half of your heart—to win, to keep going, to fight, to feel good about herself, and to conquer this battle we call life.

A WIFE'S NUMBER ONE NEED

Do you know what your wife's number one felt need is? As much as you would like it to be so, it is not sex, nor twice-daily sex. That may be what you feel is *your* number one need, but it is definitely not hers. All women in all studies in all countries and in all galaxies rank their number one need the same. It is unconditional love. Communication and emotional intimacy follow the lead of unconditional love, but these two needs provide women's number one complaint about men: "My husband isn't capable of communication and emotional intimacy."

Guys, this isn't a good thing. When our wives sense their needs for love, communication, and emotional intimacy are going unmet, the results are ugly:

- Wives withdraw from their husbands.
- Wives build low-level resentment against their husbands.
- Wives grow bitter toward their husbands.
- Wives lose sexual interest in their husbands.
- Wives begin to lose respect for their husbands.
- Wives will look elsewhere to have their needs met.

You don't want any of those nasty consequences. So one of the keys to moving toward meeting your wife's needs is found in your ability to freely dispense the power of encouragement. While your words of affirmation won't *immediately* meet the deepest need of conveying unconditional love, it is the most direct and quickest way to begin heading in the right direction.

Please don't minimize this! There is tremendous power in the intentional words of a loving husband. What types of phrases hold this power? Millions of word combinations will work as long as they are crafted from a loving heart:

- "Honey, you are smoking hot! I could just look at you all day!"
- "You have amazing ideas! I love how your mind works."
- "I love how you talk about our kids. You have such a beautiful heart!"
- "I am so grateful for you!"
- "I'm the luckiest man alive to be married to you."
- "It's so great that you don't sweat as much as you used to!" (Just kidding on that one.)

As you begin to regularly speak these types of words, you will start meeting one of your wife's deeper needs. Then if you want to really get her engine running, don't just vocalize your thoughts privately. Say them in front of others.

Yes, it takes a secure and mature man to say these types of things. Be that man! Think of your words as little gifts rolling out of your mouth. We aren't always very good at buying the right gifts for our wives, but I promise you, the gifts of encouraging words are always in season, always appropriate, and always well received. Plus, they don't cost us any money. Think about it—a free gift that can build up, bless, empower, motivate, change, inspire, and shape your wife. What a gift! The right word at the right time with the right motive will make things so right within your wife's soul. If you doubt me, consider this nugget of wisdom from the book of Proverbs: "The words of the godly are a life-giving fountain" (10:11 NLT).

Husbands, there is life-giving power waiting to be unleashed in your words.

In Gary Chapman's hugely popular book *The Five Love Languages*, he identifies words of affirmation as one of the five primary love languages that deeply connect with people. Here's his list:

- Words of Affirmation
- Quality Time
- Receiving Gifts
- Acts of Service
- Physical Touch

The premise of his book is that one of these five love languages is *the primary* way your wife feels and receives love. While they are all important, for each individual, one of the five usually reveals itself as the most powerful expression of love.[1]

When I played baseball in high school, I could throw five pitches: a fastball, a change-up, a knuckleball, a slider, and the one I threw most effectively, the home run ball, which is why I never played baseball after high school.

Your wife has one primary pitch that will give her the best chance of hitting a home run. The question is, do you know what it is? And unlike the pitcher/hitter metaphor, you want her to hit the home run. Are you throwing her *that* pitch?

If you are not sure what it is, here is a hint: your wife's primary love language is probably the one she uses most as she demonstrates love to you and others. You can usually tell which is most important by watching how she expresses love to others. The way one most naturally gives love typically will reveal how she best likes to receive love.

For me, words of affirmation tops my list—I love to receive intentional and personal affirmation, and I most commonly express love through my words. Unfortunately, words of affirmation is not my wife's primary love language. Cathy definitely values words of affirmation, and genuinely appreciates when I affirm her, but they aren't her home run pitch. She feels most loved when receiving gifts. I should have read Chapman's book earlier because it took me years to learn this truth . . . mostly the hard way.

One year I had my assistant buy Cathy a birthday gift. Bad move on my part. I don't remember why or how she caught me, but I will never forget her hurt by what I had done. I remember thinking, *What's the big deal? You got a beautiful necklace. Who cares about who actually made the purchase?* But as it turned out, Cathy cared. She cared deeply. With her primary love language being receiving gifts, it is never the gift itself that conveys love to Cathy; it is the thought behind the gift. In this case the message she received was *Doug is too busy, and I'm not important enough for him to be bothered with his buying me a gift himself.*

Gulp. Bad message.

Another year *I went out on my own* and bought Cathy a calendar for her birthday. I thought it would help motivate her to become timelier and help her productivity around the house. Mea culpa. Yeah, it didn't go over well, and I hate to admit that I was stupid enough to think that maybe the issue was that she didn't like the design of the calendar, so I immediately went out and bought her a *cuter* one. Fortunately, I had a whole year to figure out that a calendar wasn't a good idea. (Note to self: gifts that "send a message" usually send the wrong message.)

Your wife's love language matters! Search for the main one, but you will do your marriage a favor by becoming proficient at them all. So go to school on her ASAP!

Think of it this way: When you are trying to build muscle, you have to add protein to your diet. Protein comes in many different forms, such as soy, beef, turkey, chicken, pork, fish, or protein powder (just don't leave any on the counter). All are helpful to build muscle. As husbands, we have to find ways to build marriage muscles to help our wives win. Your wife is starving for the protein only you can give her.

So fill up your wife's plate with powerful words. Just think of each affirmation as an ounce of protein on her empty plate. Consider her hungry for affirmation, and remember it is within your power to feed her well. Check out how this idea is phrased in Proverbs: "Wise words satisfy like a good meal; the right words bring satisfaction" (18:20 NLT).

FOUR IDEAS TOWARD HEROISM
WITH YOUR WORDS

So, practically speaking, how do we become more affirming in what we say to our wives? Here are four ideas you can immediately put into practice with your wife that will help you along the path toward heroism.

1. If you think something positive, say it.

- "You look beautiful today."
- "I love how comfortable our home is."
- "That was a great meal."
- "I love seeing you in the morning!"
- "It's amazing how friendly you are to strangers. You have a beautiful heart."

I realize this will be really difficult for some of you. Plus, I may be making it a little confusing too. Last chapter I told you *not* to say what you are thinking. Now I'm telling you to express it when you think it. This is kind of like mental juggling—one ball is good, and the other is bad (don't go there). The key difference is that one builds up, and the other tears down. Blessed is the hero who discerns the difference. To become a pro at juggling your words, you are going to need to practice. This new expression of vocabulary won't just appear by watching TV; you will need real-life experiences to try it out. This may come to feel as if you are learning a second language, and that's not fun. There also will be times when you won't feel like affirming your wife, but you will need to do it anyway! To be a hero with your words, you need to practice, practice, and practice.

As you are developing this new skill, be prepared that your wife may not offer any affirming comments back to you. She may be stunned. She may be waiting to see if it sticks once you put this book down. She may be too wounded to engage in this type of intimacy. That's okay. Genuine encouragement isn't given with the expectation of getting affirmation in return. So don't expect it. It doesn't matter. If you haven't been affirming her regularly along the way, she has been starving for that encouragement protein for so long that it may take weeks before she is full enough and has any strength to share some leftovers with you.

2. Set yourself a reminder.

If you are like me, you find it difficult to remember important things without lists and reminders. As you are practicing this skill, it's okay to do something that will aid in triggering your memory. In addition to old-fashioned pen and paper, today's technology makes setting reminders so easy.

If you have an iPhone, you can have Siri set a daily reminder for you:

> **ME:** Please remind me three times every day to tell Cathy something I love about her.
> **SIRI:** Okay, I'll start reminding you.
> **ME:** Am I the man for doing this?
> **SIRI:** I'd rather not say.
> **ME:** Ouch. Come on, Siri, who's the man?
> **SIRI:** You the man.
> **ME:** Thanks!
> **SIRI:** I am programmed to please.

Guys, become more like Siri. Aim to please your wives. Set a reminder, and develop the habit of affirming her each day.

Soon the love in your heart will bubble up, and your words will roll out so naturally that you won't need reminders. But until then, remind yourself.

3. Text it when you think it; affirmation doesn't always have to be verbal.

I try to flirt with my wife all day long via text. I find it's just a simple way to stay connected to Cathy throughout the day in a way that assures her she is always on my mind.

I'm thinking about you right now . . .

I love you . . .

I miss you . . .

I can't wait to see you . . .

I had some casaba melons for lunch and thought of you . . .

4. Notes: When you think it, write it.

Become a pro at writing notes to your wife. Pick up some sticky notes or a package of note cards (I recently bought a package of one hundred colorful notes and envelopes at Target for nine dollars). Then whenever something positive comes to mind for which you can affirm your wife, write a short note (it doesn't have to be an essay) and leave it in a creative place for her to find later (and still be pleasantly surprised). Tape it to the toilet seat, sneak it into her pocketbook, place it on the dashboard of her car in the middle of the night, hide it in the ice tray, or attach it to the dog. This results in a double-win of thoughtfulness.

Writing notes of affirmation is not normal for most husbands. Normal for us runs more to the skills of poking fun or making witty, sarcastic, or condescending comments. It may be right in our wheelhouse to goof around and use put-downs, but wives don't appreciate it when we use those skills on them. They don't like punches in the arm either. "Hey baby!" *[Punch!]* won't earn you any more points today with your wife than it did in junior high—and neither will writing snarky notes.

Look men, we want to become less sucky in life. Many of us try hard to become masters of our domains, whether we are talking about work, investing, or sports. To get better, we practice. It is no different in marriage when it comes to becoming proficient at encouraging our wives. We have to practice.

Please start practicing this today. You can do it! We can help our wives (and ourselves too) win in life when we let them know throughout the day that they are not alone and that the other halves of their hearts are crazy about them, madly in love with them, and cheering them on!

4B

BUT WHAT ABOUT ME?

I heard a pastor once say to a group of men, "As a husband, always remember: God meets your needs, not your wife." Here endeth the sermon.

A couple years later I heard that same pastor not only had an affair with his assistant (why is it always the assistant?) but left the ministry and his family to marry her.

Obviously, God was not meeting *all* of his needs.

A wise and experienced friend of mine told me something I have never forgotten: "God fills the God parts we need. But humans were designed to fill the human parts."

We are desperate for human connection, and yet we miss those opportunities with our spouses on a regular basis. I have just challenged you to connect with your wife through words. But what if encouraging words don't come your way? Do you even notice? Do you care? Really?

When I walk by strangers, I smile and say, "Hi." About 75 percent of the time this greeting is met with the response of, "Fine." What? All I said was hi. I didn't ask a question. I assume they think I'm going to say, "How's it going?" or "How are you?" or "How's that melanoma on your neck?" I'm saying one thing, and they are hearing another. I don't know if it is the tone I use with my simple greeting or if they are transfixed on my seductive receding hairline or if they are shocked that someone with my appearance could snag such a beautiful wife. Regardless, it's a miss.

In a similar fashion to my hi–fine scenario, that is what seems to happen when I talk to men about "say what is powerful." Guys are eager to try it out on their wives—which I appreciate and applaud—but they are less concerned with and can easily dismiss their own need for these life-giving words from their wives. It is a strange dynamic. It's not that they don't value words; they just place a higher value on having their physical needs being met. I get it. I may be a "words guy," but that doesn't take away my need to connect through physical intimacy.

Women will tell me, "I sure hope my husband was paying attention to your material on affirmation. His words are few, but when he encourages me, I come alive." Honestly, I can't ever remember a time when a guy has said that to me about his wife after a speaking engagement. When men talk about what they hope their wives heard from one of my speeches, it is always related to having their physical needs met.

So with that reality in mind, let's switch this up a little. Let's move from the need to connect with words to the need to connect through physical intimacy. Instead of asking, "What do I do if my wife is not affirming me?" let's consider how to get *your* "love needs" met without being selfish, demanding, and stupid.

First, this battle will be impossible to fight if your wife hasn't fully bought into the fact that she and she alone is God's provision for your physical intimacy needs. Other folks can buy you gifts. They can affirm nice things about your character. They can engage you in spending quality (platonic) time. They can do little things to serve you.

But no one else is designed to meet your need for physical touch, especially the physical *sexual* touch you occasionally think about (every eighteen seconds for most men, last time I checked). One guy I know had completely given up on ever getting his physical needs met from his wife and convinced himself sex was "a drive that could be channeled to other areas of attention," as opposed to a God-given need that required fulfillment. His marriage ended after an affair (surprise, surprise).

I would like to rationalize that the twenty-first century is way different from previous centuries, that because we live in an oversexualized society, we have it much tougher than the guys in biblical times.

But then I read the Bible.

Men apparently have been malfunctioning in the sexual area for . . . ever!

Okay, so the Internet has fed the beast a bit more of late than it did during the apostle Paul's era. And there is no doubt the dopamine fix of porn can make us just as addicted to sex as a cocaine user is addicted to expensive white powder. But in reality, today's sexual culture has simply made more pronounced the need we already had.

So, yes, a wife needs to know all this. She needs to know what pressures we are under, where we are weakest, and how much we need to feel like men in sexual ways. She must completely understand men and sex and why the two shall never be separated on this earth. Chances are good that though she claimed to have bought this book as a gift for you, in reality she had her own agenda in mind for areas she wanted to see change, so don't be afraid to have her read this section (after you've practiced for a good amount of time saying what is powerful), and take this discussion to a deeper place within your marriage. Don't be that guy who gives up because his wife doesn't give in.

Second, we as men cannot afford to be juvenile about getting our way. "My wife won't meet my physical touch needs, so I'm entitled to meet them on my own or have someone else meet them for me" (aka *pornography and masturbation*).

Sadly, this reasoning is a reality for many men—even Christians. And my guess is about 95 percent of men have failed in this area (and the other 5 percent are lying). They have failed so much that they have given up.

Look: whole books are being written about this issue, and my sense is most men ought to read all of them. We are losing this battle and giving up. Normal guys, pastors, pro athletes, computer programmers, every demographic and job that could possibly be represented is a player in this game.

My best encouragement for you today is this: Stay in the battle. Don't give up.

There is daily forgiveness. And if you ask God right now, He will wipe away the past (read Psalm 51). You have today to start over, and it is a good day to do so. You can't change or fix the past, and you can't live today thinking the future holds more failure (read Matt. 6:9–13; Luke 11:1–4). All you have is today. Battle today; say no to the lying voice in your brain, asking you to feed your natural desires with pornography, then act them out in ways that damage your soul and the soul of your marriage.

Third, ask yourself if you are so sexually selfish and unrealistic in your sexual expectations that your wife could never in a million years meet your fake standards of what it will take to meet your physical-sexual touch needs. Too many guys have taken the easy way out by feasting on porn and have created idealistic impressions of what a woman can and should do. My brother, please hear me: that is not a woman you've been watching—she is an actress, and I would bet anything that her real life isn't anything like her film life. Get real! Your fantasy life is destroying your marriage.

God asks us to renew our minds in dozens of places in the Bible (most notably Romans 12). How is your mind? Does it need to be renewed? To be her hero, we need to become aggressive at holding up the mirror and looking within to determine whether we are half the problem. If so, we have to get help to overcome our own issues *before* (yes, before) we expect our wives to change in the bedroom. Nothing says disingenuous so much as the man who is choosing to lose the battle every day, then blaming his wife because of his lack of self-control. You did not marry a porn star. Get that false picture out of your mind, ask Jesus to renew and restore your mind, and begin working on these heroic actions.

Fourth, once you have had a few months of consistent battle victories, you must have the hardest conversation of your life. And perhaps it needs to happen in the safety of a counselor's office. Your wife needs to look in her own mirror and ponder whether she can step up to the plate, and if not, why she cannot. Perhaps she has low hormone levels (usually estrogen or progesterone) that could be fixed with a quick and painless blood draw and then the right prescription. (The research on the chemicals and hormones we ingest over the years and how they affect our own hormones is in: too much of *this* and not enough of *that* has changed our hormonal makeup in large doses. It may be time to get rebalanced. And you won't know until you get some blood work done.) Maybe she has abuse issues in her past that need healing. It is conceivable you are so anxious and insistent on having your needs met that you do not care or have a darn clue how to hit her spot to help her get to bingo, and she has given up ever thinking you will care to try.

Maybe all four. Whatever it is, you must dig for this answer as though it was a hundred million dollars buried in your backyard. Whether it's your issue or hers, this is an area you *must* talk about and work on until it is solved. You cannot go years living in secrets and frustration. It is bad for your heart, her heart . . . the One Heart God wants you to have. It will likely end your marriage at the worst possible time (when your kids are still at home and need you both).

Be her hero though she may not recognize that is what you are really trying to be. Protect your marriage in this most important area, and you have a chance to be her hero her whole life.

5

ACTION #3:
DON'T SAY ANYTHING!
(OR BECOME A WORLD-CLASS LISTENER)

A t this point in the book, I know some guys are thinking, *I can see why my wife bought me this book and how all this stuff will be helpful to my marriage, but I still need more advice about sex.*

I understand that you might be reading this because you want some more practical, hands-on tips to improve your sex life. Here is my take on the big picture in this important area for most men: learning and mastering the skills to become a better husband will absolutely lead to an improved sex life. You might not think that improving communication with your wife is very sexy, but your wife does. In fact, one of the reasons you may not be having sex as much as you would like is because you are not a good listener; your wife doesn't feel connected and emotionally intimate with you, so why would she want to be physically intimate? I know. You've heard that scenario before, right? Yeah, me too! A lot of us guys find it easy to hear things but tough to really listen.

To many women, a good listener is *sexy*. Asking questions that trigger conversation is like romantic foreplay to your wife, especially if you follow through and listen well. Do you want to be her hero? Become a world-class listener!

There are two primary reasons why husbands typically suck at listening:

1. We talk too much and dominate conversations with our wives. What they say is largely background noise or the platform we need to make *our* points.
2. We don't seem to care enough to really listen to our wives. We especially haven't mastered the important skill of digging a little deeper so they talk *even more*.

Both are *huge* problems.

Let's start with the first reason and take a look at Mr. Talks-a-lot.

MR. TALKS-A-LOT

It is difficult to construct a quality marriage with a man who talks a lot and doesn't listen. I know some people (and so do you) who start to talk and ramble on, and they have *no clue* that I have truly checked out. I could actually leave the conversation, run a 10K, shower, and come back, and they would still be talking—without ever noticing that I had left. If you don't know someone like that, *beware.* It may be *you!*

How can you tell if you are Mr. Talks-a-lot? Here are a few signs:

1. When you talk to your wife, her eyes glaze over into a dull, vacant, unfocused stare. Her pupils are fixed and dilated.
2. You find yourself having to physically restrain your wife to prevent her from walking away while you speak.
3. When you are talking, your wife holds up her phone that never rang and says, "I have to take this call."
4. You are talking, and your wife is snoring. Yikes. Bad sign.
5. Your wife has to occasionally wipe your spit off her arm when you are talking to her.

Here is a general relationship principle: no one is interested in being in a relationship with a world-class talker.

To make the move from being a world-class talker to a world-class listener, you must discipline yourself to shut off your internal dialogue engine. This is the mechanism that makes you want to come up with the next thing to say while your wife is speaking or brings to mind the ways you want to correct her or fix her or calm her down. Turning this engine off can be difficult, but it is necessary to improve your listening skills, to be intellectually present when your wife is speaking, and to actually be able to make an emotional connection when listening.

If you are a world-class talker, you have to learn to stop interrupting your wife when she talks. This will take patience and practice.

Here is some biblical wisdom that addresses this idea of listening and is absolutely fundamental to building a quality marriage: "Post this at all the intersections, dear friends: Lead with your ears, follow up with your tongue, and let anger straggle along in the rear" (James 1:19 MSG).

When I follow this biblical advice, it communicates a very powerful message to Cathy. It says, "You are important to me. You have something worth saying, and regardless of whether I find the content of your words interesting, you are valuable enough to engage my ears, my heart, and my body." Wives are hungry to feel this type of value from their husbands. I hear their complaints all the time: *I want him to care enough to want to listen.*

Some time ago I was at a pharmacy, waiting for a prescription. (I'm fine now, thanks. The tapeworms are all gone.) I met a woman while waiting in line who started talking to me and never stopped. I hadn't met anyone who could actually talk without breathing, but this woman had mad skills! By the time I left, I think I knew more about this woman than I know about my own wife. As I reflected on this encounter, I began to wonder about her husband: *Does he even allow her to talk at home? Is she so desperate for someone to listen that strangers are a welcome audience?* It seemed obvious that this woman was missing something from her man.

What about your wife? Are you giving her the audience she

needs? Are you aware that there are times when she needs you to be the recipient of her words and heart?

When my kids were young, I would occasionally come home from work to find my wife locked in the bathroom. She wasn't constipated; she was escaping and hiding from the kids. You see, she would reach a limit when she was maxed out with kids-who-talk-about-nothing-or-nonsense-and-can-do-it-forever-and-have-no-idea-they're-driving-their-amazingly-patient-mom-totally-crazy. She'd had enough! She needed immediate quiet and adult conversation as soon as possible. Are you aware when your wife needs some you-time? It may not be as obvious as an AWOL toilet scenario, but you can be your wife's hero when you are simply there and willing to listen—and if you listen well.

I have many regrets over things I have said to my wife in thirty-plus years of marriage. I can actually grieve when I recall misplaced and hurtful words that I have used. But I have *no regrets* over listening to Cathy. I have never thought, *Why did I pay so much attention to what she said? Why was I so patient and empathetic and interested?* Listening never leads to regrets!

Here is the bottom line for Mr. Talks-a-lot: if you talk too much, it is absolutely destroying intimacy, and it needs to (and can) be identified, addressed, and fixed.

Next, let's take a look at the more common husband, the one who doesn't like to talk—or listen.

MR. NO-TALK

It is also next to impossible to experience a quality marriage when the husband has an aversion to communication. This guy may have master skills in grunting "uh-huh" and in giving short responses ("Good," "Fine," "Did you buy beer?"), but he doesn't care to engage in conversation. Likewise, he doesn't listen well because listening often requires paying the cost of having to focus attention outside of himself and of having to respond and verbally participate with his spouse. This guy can often be found hiding out in the safety of his hobbies or in his man cave.

What leads to becoming a Mr. No-Talk? There can be many factors: a nagging wife, a history of arguments, living with a Mrs. Talks-a-lot, or strong degrees of apathy and self-centeredness. The good news is that if you are a Mr. No-Talk you, too, can change to become more effective at communication and be a better husband.

Real change starts with making an intentional decision to break out of the cocoon of isolation for the sake of your marriage and family. Then begin taking action to become focused in your interaction with your wife to become a better communicator and a better listener. Here are three doable action steps you can immediately begin to work on:

1. **Ask additional questions.** Asking the simple prompter question "How was your day?" is one of the best ways for me to engage Cathy and express my interest. I don't even have to follow up with "Tell me more about it" anymore.

The initial simple question is enough to start the engine and accelerate the conversation. What follows is what poor listeners would say is the difficult part of the conversation: focusing on her words and hearing her heart behind the words. While you listen, don't think of ways to fix the situation or end the conversation; instead craft an additional question you can ask in order to deepen the level of conversation (again, this is very sexy). A response like, "Oh, that sounds nice, honey," doesn't lead to any further discussion. In fact, it cuts it off. Developing the skill of asking good follow-up questions (yes, it is a learned skill) will go a long way to improving your communication health. For example, "So what did you do when Johnny hid his bubble gum in Shaggy's fur?" is the type of question that expresses interest and leads to more conversation.

2. **Pay attention to your body language.** Communication science tells us that only 45 percent of a message is communicated verbally, while 55 percent is communicated through body language. Make no mistake: your body language sends a message. It tells the person speaking to you that you are either engaged and care or disinterested and don't care. For example, when your wife is talking and you engage in good eye contact and your facial expression shows interest, you are sending the message, *Tell me more; you're important enough to listen to, and I value you.* If, on the other hand, you are facing away when your wife is talking, looking through

the day's mail pile, checking your e-mail, texting someone, or glancing over her shoulder to catch a score on *Sports Center*, you are sending the message, *I may be here physically, but I've got more important things to do than listening to you.* Whenever my wife starts talking to me (okay, 80 percent of the time), I either physically or mentally press pause on the remote so that all distractions stop. I've had to learn to discipline myself and move my body and eyes to face her, and then I practice the essential man-skill of "undivided attention," which is when number 3 kicks in.

3. **Be available.** Your wife's perception of your availability is just as important as your actual availability. If you are not the type who takes notes or highlights when you read, please reread that last sentence. It's a game-changer. Her perception of you is her reality. You may think you are the Jesus Jr. of listening, but if *she* doesn't think you are, you're not. You may be at home together, but if you are always engaged in something else—from watching television, to puttering in the garage, to playing video games, to tinkering with your investments, to surfing the Web, you are sending the wrong message to your wife, who perceives you as unavailable. You might as well hang a sign around your neck that reads, "I'm just not that into you."

Frankly, one of the problems with technology, especially smartphones, is that while they may make us look smart for work, they are making us dumb husbands. If we are always connected to work while at home, we are under-connecting with our families. I have read that more than 90 percent of all texts are returned within thirty seconds, which means we are always "on call." We have come to look, notice, check, and respond every time we get a text, whether we are at the dinner table or in bed. I have heard guys admit to checking texts during sex. *Are they crazy?!* Again, these behaviors communicate an unhealthy message to our wives. It says, "*This* is just as important as *you.*"

I'm sorry, but if you are having sex with your wife, there are not many things in life that can possibly be as important (aside from a house on fire, a child on fire, or your pet spontaneously combusting into flames), and texting should never be on that list.

For Mr. No-Talk, learning some good communication skills can be a challenge, but for most men these skills are certainly within their reach and can result in becoming better husbands and having healthier marriages. Yet talking—in and of itself—is not enough. What matters most is the type of talk you engage in.

In Gary Smalley's book *Secrets to Lasting Love: Uncovering the Keys to Life-Long Intimacy*, he describes five different levels of talking. These levels progress from the least intimate and move toward intimacy. As you read through the following brief descriptions of each level, evaluate where your normal communication would fit, and then make the effort to move to the next level. Here they are:

1. **Speaking in clichés.** Sure, this is a verbal form of com-
munication, but clichés don't really communicate any-
thing of value.
   - Hi.
   - How are you?
   - I'm fine.
   - How's it going?
   - It's all good.
   - Nice weather we're having.
   - Cool.
   - House on fire!

2. **Sharing facts.** A lot of marriages never get past com-
municating facts to one another.
   - The garbage disposal is broken again.
   - Amber pooped her pants again at school.
   - I'm tired.
   - The electric bill is twice as high as it was last
     month.
   - I saw Linda at the gym today. It looks like she's
     growing a moustache.

3. **Sharing opinions.** This is where you actually begin
sharing your opinions with your spouse. This moves
communication beneath the surface issues of life, and
you begin to become vulnerable to your wife.
   - I hate my boss. He's such a jerk.
   - We've got to figure out a way to keep Johnny from

putting his bubble gum in Shaggy's fur. What do
you think we should do?

• I really think that new paint color in the kitchen
brightens the space.

• I'm thinking that we should feed Amber less fiber
in her diet.

4. **Sharing feelings.** Okay, this one gets difficult for many
guys because we tend to be better thinkers than feel-
ers. Typically men think first, and our feelings follow a
distant second. Yet 90 percent of women feel something
first and then eventually get to think about it after feeling it. So whenever we can communicate our feelings,
the chances of really connecting with our wives go way
up. Sharing feelings is what moves our marriages into
the intimacy realm. *Note:* When something goes wrong
in her world, resist the urge to break into her quiet by
saying, "What are you thinking right now?" Chances
are high your wife isn't thinking; she's primarily *feeling.*
You'll do better with these types of questions:

• How are you feeling about that situation with
your mother?

• What are you sensing we need to talk to Mary
about before she goes out with Luke Friday night?

• How are you feeling about our plans for vacation
this summer?

• What are your instincts telling you about how
many sports Brittany ought to play this year?

- I can't believe that I married such a wonderful woman—I feel like the luckiest guy in the world.
- It sure makes me feel great when you wear that old cheerleader outfit and shake your pom-poms.

5. **Sharing needs.** This fifth level is the most intimate type of communication. It is where we begin to reveal and discuss our desires and needs.

- I want so much for us to have a stronger marriage.
- I am totally bored with my job. I need to start looking for something that better fits my skills.
- I need to do a better job communicating with you, and I need your help to hold me accountable.
- I'd really love for us to carve out some time to talk about our sex life and revisit our expectations.[1]

If we are honest, most of us guys are fine staying at the cliché, fact, and opinion levels of communication. Men can stay at these levels forever with the guys we call our best friends. But we also need to understand this: our wives *want* and *need* more from us. They need us to communicate at deep and intimate levels, and learning to become good listeners is the key to being successful in this arena. True, our wives can never force us to go deeper in communication. It is not natural for us to go deep. We have to make the decision that it is worth doing. We have to learn the skills, practice them, and master them. You *can* do this!

Men, I hope you see this as a worthwhile investment. Good communication is so important and foundational to building and maintaining a healthy marriage. Becoming a world-class listener will go a long way to decrease your suckiness quotient and raise your status as a husband who has become her hero.

——— 5B ———

HELPING HER DO THE MATH

Yes, two ears and one mouth mean we ought to listen twice as much as talk, right? Well, when women have the twenty-thousand-words-a-day need going (a man's is about five thousand), sometimes the balance of airtime is off-kilter. What do you do when *you* are the one who needs a listening ear and she hasn't mastered that skill or didn't get that spiritual gift?

"Shut up and listen for a change, would ya?" likely won't get you to the desired goal of being heard. So if her constant barrage of words comes without a clue as to how to listen, it is time to hand her a quarter so she can buy one. Nicely, and without snark or abuse.

Sandwich time again:

"Honey, I love to hear you talk. Your voice is one of the things I fell in love with—along with all of the other parts—when we were first going out. But . . .

"Sometimes I need someone to listen to me, and I really

want it to be you. I often *feel* like you don't recognize that I may need to talk too. What can I do to signal to you that I need some airtime to talk?

"You're such a great wife in a hundred different areas, and I love listening to you and your heart, but this is one area where I need a little more of you. I'd so much rather talk deeply with you than any of my friends."

Other possible statements at this point, depending on your dilemma, might be . . .

"Honey, I love to hear you talk. Your voice is one of the things I fell in love with—along with all of the other parts—when we were first going out. But . . .

"When we're having a discussion, my mind can only take a few minutes of what you're trying to say; then it starts to wander. I desperately want to get better at this. Maybe it's because of the thousands of hours of video games I played when I was a teenager that I have a little bit of ADHD. Since I want to hear and understand the things you're saying, you may need to take a break for a minute or two; let me repeat back what I just heard so you know I'm really listening; then let me ask a question or two to clarify what you just said. That works better than long monologues of important info you don't want me to miss. Does that make sense?

"I really love your mother and wish she would visit more often. And did I tell you how much I like your shoes?

You're such a good shopper, and I wish you'd spend more money on yourself."

Or . . .

"Honey, I love to hear you talk. Your voice is one of the things I fell in love with—along with all of the other parts— when we were first going out. But . . .

"I need to vent about my day a bit. And you know how when you vent I immediately try to fix it by giving you advice about what to do or not do? Well, I'm sorry I do that sometimes; I'm a man and I. Must. Fix. Things. I'm trying to change that about myself. But I need you to let me talk first and get it all out so I don't lose my train of thought before you jump in. Then when I need your advice about something particular, I'll ask you a specific question.

"Have I told you lately that you may be the best cook on the planet and without you I literally would be dead? And I really love the color of paint we have in the kitchen. You should be an interior decorator!"

(No, you don't have to go over the top with the sandwich method, but I know that we guys need practical examples. No extra charge. You're welcome.)

If you don't calmly clarify expectations when it comes to back-and-forth conversations, then you are essentially expecting her to read your mind. How does that work when she expects that out of you? Exactly! Never works.

So if you need her to listen and all she wants to do is hear her own voice, you really may need to find a way to put the conversation on hold, tell her what you need at that particular moment, then hope she is able to listen.

If you want to be her long-term hero, the goal should be to help her be a better listener without shaming or demeaning her. While most women are nurturers by nature and are therefore great listeners, some didn't get that gene or never saw it modeled during their childhoods. By lovingly helping her give ear to your needs, you are protecting your marriage for the long haul of life and love.

6

ACTION #4:
GO BIG WITH SMALL THINGS

Two men walk onto a bridge about ten feet above a river. Both need to take a leak. As they are taking care of their business, one man says to the other: "Wow, that river is cold." The other, not missing a beat, replies, "Yeah, and it's deep too."

Size jokes start early in life and apparently never get old. When my dad was in his seventies, he was debilitated by Parkinson's disease. But he still had his wit. I remember him one day shuffling up to a short urinal and saying, "I'm using this one because I need a little more distance." This from a man who drooled and couldn't walk by himself anymore. Dad knew how to make me laugh; he was simply playing into the cultural-male-gag about size. Guys are conditioned to believe that size matters.

I want to set the record straight. When it comes to your

relationship with your wife, size does matter. All research points to the fact that women prefer small. This may come as a relief to you 99-percenters, and you might be thinking, *Thank God. What a relief.* Unfortunately for you, I'm not referring to *that*!

Women prefer that their husbands become proficient at mastering the small but meaningful acts of service that are the building blocks to any strong marriage. Small acts of kindness, service, and initiative all add up to a big deal.

I am convinced that most marriages that have drifted apart have done so because one or both spouses stopped doing the small things that really matter.

You might be tempted to think, *Doug, I've got some serious issues in my marriage, and you're making juvenile jokes and telling me to do small stuff? I need to do something that brings big change, or my marriage is in a serious world of hurt.*

I get it. But here's the real story: the neglect of doing little things is likely what led to the big issues, and *it is* the little things that can lead to big change!

I was meeting with a friend recently who told me, "My marriage is in trouble. It used to be really good, but I've noticed that we've stopped doing some of the basic, small things that were once so meaningful. What do you think we should do?"

It would have been easy to whip out the default reply, "Get some counseling." At times, counseling is a very good idea. But in this case my friend actually knew the *why* about the cause of his deteriorating marriage, so the answer was obvious: "Start doing the little things!"

Small, basic actions are often the key to success in marriage. When we stop doing the small things, our marriages can end up in places we never intended to take them. Think of it this way: if a ship sets out on a long journey just one degree off course, over time it will end up radically missing its destination. That's a perfect metaphor of what happens in marriage when the *small acts* go missing.

When I've counseled older couples in trouble, those with a couple of decades behind them in marriage, invariably they can point to the early years in marriage, when one (usually both) got off course by just a small degree. And then after twenty-plus years of being off course by one degree, they are not only on different planets but in different solar systems. Those marriages will require a great deal of work to bring them back to where the rockets are able to fly in tandem again. Much more than it would have been had they started earlier by doing the small acts of service and making minor midcourse corrections to keep them going toward their desired destinations.

When it comes to marriage, some of you have missed your destination because you have neglected the small acts of serving your spouse. My advice is that you change your course and start doing the small things—regularly—and you will find that your marriage will be on the pathway to becoming stronger and healthier. I know this is true because every relationship I have seen succeed is fueled by acts of sacrificial serving. Serving the other half of your heart is a sign of depth and connection.

Now, if I'm being brutally honest with myself (and you), I will have to admit that serving others (my wife included) does not come naturally. My first instinct is usually to wait until others serve me. I prefer that posture the best. (Perhaps this is why I find myself waiting so often.) I don't think I'm alone in this. I have a hunch that I am a lot like most guys. So if we are going to serve our wives, the first step is to acknowledge that our natural inclination and preference is selfishness.

So please repeat after me:

ME: "I am severely selfish."
YOU: "I am severely selfish."

There. Don't you feel better? I know I do.

Once we have faced this ugly truth about ourselves, then we can understand that something within us needs to change.

Definition of *change*: a humbling experience we can do internally before anyone has to tell us or our actions sabotage us, thus incurring no embarrassment in front of the wife or friends and, in fact, incurring the admiration of said wife and others because they see maturity in action. Or *change*: a humbling experience that can hit us over the head after we've allowed our pride to hold its ground until our selfish and adolescent actions become obvious to all, and we have to humble ourselves anyway if we want to save the relationships we most care about.

Tough choice.

The challenge for making the right decision involving how we are going to change is this: selfishness is flat out too easy! We don't have to be smart to be selfish. We just need to be breathing.

If you happen to be one of those I'm-holier-than-you

Christians, please get over yourself. You are not. Just because you are a Christian or have been one for a long time does not automatically mean you have mastered and done away with all selfishness.

Time to get real.

Here is what Jesus had to continually teach His closest followers:

> "You know that in this world kings are tyrants, and officials lord it over the people beneath them. But among you it should be quite different. Whoever wants to be a leader among you must be your servant, and whoever wants to be first must become your slave. For even I, the Son of Man, came here not to be served but to serve others, and to give my life as a ransom for many." (Matt. 20:25–28 NLT)

I think Jesus' choice to use the word *slave* is interesting. In our culture *slave* carries an extremely negative connotation because slaves were captive to an evil, human system. But in Jesus' spiritual system, we are not captive and forced to serve against our will. We are free to choose what we do. Yet it is through the exercising of this freedom that we choose to serve as a demonstration of our love for God.

So the key to a better relationship with your wife begins with settling the battle going on in yourself, wrestling with the question, Will I obey Jesus and serve, or will I obey what comes naturally and serve myself?

We can talk about loving our wives all we want, but the real proof is not found in our words. It is not found in what we spend on a weekend away from the kids, nor is it found in something shiny we bought because we think that a *big* purchase makes up for missing out on a lot of small acts of service. The real proof is found in our actions. A great Bible verse that captures this concept reads, "Dear children, let us stop just saying we love each other; let us really show it by our actions" (1 John 3:18 NLT).

Let me meddle in your life for a minute by asking you a couple of questions: When was the last time your actions showed how much you love your wife? When did you stop whatever you were doing to make the effort to do something that was inconvenient or uncomfortable in order to serve your wife—and you did it without grumbling or complaining (and without expectation of a "reward")?

The way you answer those questions is a good tool for you to use to evaluate how you are doing in the area of serving. Keep in mind that a relationship that has "serve" in its equation isn't about the big stuff. Rather, it's all about the small stuff.

One night I was headed for bed and noticed while walking past the kitchen counter that Cathy had left her phone downstairs. She was upstairs getting ready for bed. Two thoughts came to mind: (1) She'd want her phone because she relies on the alarm in the morning. (2) If I didn't bring it upstairs with me, she'd have to get out of bed later once she realized she left it downstairs. So I was faced with the question: What should Doug Fields do? *On the one hand*, I thought, *it would serve her right to have to get up and go downstairs to get it herself. After all, she could have picked up my cup of Diet Coke from her car, and we all know how that turned out! On the other hand, I could decide right here and now to serve her in this small way by bringing her phone upstairs so she won't have to retrieve it later.* In the end I did the right thing. It was truly such a little act that took no real effort on my part. But Cathy was *so* thankful that I had done this tiny, miniscule act of service.

The big acts you might be tempted to think most about—buying her a car, jewelry, or an outfit or expensive vacation—don't require you to be a servant. What is most empowering to a relationship are not the onetime or occasional extravagant acts but the many, many small ones.

Small actions that can add up to making huge differences in your relationship are everywhere, just waiting to happen:

- going out to dinner where *she* wants to go
- knowing her favorite radio station and turning it on when she is in the car with you
- bringing home her favorite drink . . . just because
- getting out of bed to turn off the light when she was last to bed
- helping her find her keys when she has lost them
- helping her put away the groceries
- giving her the last bite of your lunch
- doing some of her normal tasks without being asked
- offering, "Let me get that for you"

- volunteering, "I know it's your day to drive the kids to school, but let me do it"

Here is a bonus tip: do not offer to perform an act of service for your wife and then suggest that she do something else instead. I will not confirm or deny that any of these have ever happened in my home, but I strongly suggest that you don't say them:

- "Let me do the dishes so you can go jogging and work off that meal you just ate."
- "I'll play with the kids. This way you can go clean that gross toilet in our bathroom."
- "You look all sweaty. How about I put the kids to bed so you can go shower? When I finish, I'll join you."

Here is some encouragement: you can move your marriage back on course if you master the art of doing the little things. Like everything else I have mentioned in the previous chapters, this also takes practice. Start today by performing at least one small sacrificial act of service for your wife. Then try to do one every day. As doing the small things becomes part of your daily routine, I promise that your wife won't think you suck as much as you once did.

And you *will* continue in the direction of being her hero.

6B

More of the Sword So You "Get the Point"

Who serves more in your relationship? Who is doing more of the small stuff to keep the house in order, the kids well cared for, and the food prepared and on the table?

If you answer that question honestly and still come up with "me," well, you are a better man than I am. But if you immediately went to, "Well, I'm gone nine or ten hours a day to make the dough so she can make the bread and do all of these servant-type things," then I would like you to do a little Bible study on servanthood. In fact, we can start now with the four passages that follow.

Passage One: "For even the Son of Man did not come to be served, but to serve, and to give his life as a ransom for many" (Mark 10:45).

This is a here-endeth-the-discussion passage. If our goal is to go through this life boot camp to learn how to become more like Jesus, then this is our job description. No, we don't have to give our lives as ransom for many. Only One needed to do that. But His whole attitude was serving, not being served. You will never be more like Jesus than when you serve.

It doesn't take a Dr. Phil to quickly realize that entitlement is the killer of relationships. Think about people at work, at church, in college . . . you know, those folks out there who think the world owes them a great job, lots of cash, and plenty of leisure time. The entitled in our world are the most selfish people on the planet. And the most unhappy. Nothing satisfies them, they are bored with it all, and they only have the brain space to think about themselves. If all of the unhappy people in the world do one thing—find a way to serve someone besides themselves—they are likely not to be unhappy for long.

Serving others frees us from the prison of our selfishness. In fact, I will go so far as to say it is the *only* key that unlocks true happiness in any relationship.

Why?

It was the key Jesus used when He came into this world. "The Son of Man did not come to be served, but to serve."

Passage Two: "Each of you should use whatever gift you have received to serve others, as faithful stewards of God's grace in its various forms" (1 Peter 4:10).

What gifts do you have? Let's think outside the standard gifts for a moment. You have . . .

- the gift of time,
- the gift of knowing what your wife needs to make her world better and having it in your power to give it, and

- the gift of being a Christ-following man who understands the power of servanthood within a relationship (right?).

A husband's faithful stewardship within his marriage constantly asks, "What can I do for her?" Even more so, you can ask, "What can I do for the other half of my heart?"

Passage Three: "Serve wholeheartedly, as if you were serving the Lord, not people, because you know that the Lord will reward each one for whatever good they do" (Eph. 6:7–8).

All serving is serving Jesus. So maybe it is time we switch the question from, "How can I serve my wife?" to "How can I serve Jesus within this relationship?" And if we serve with right motives, some sort of reward is promised. The reward is not the goal, of course, but it does seem to promise that our serving is not in vain. Was Christ's service to the planet in vain? No. Was it hard? Yes. Was it worth it? A big yes.

If we serve the Lord, we leave the distribution of rewards to Him. Our reward is (finally) learning what it means to do what Jesus would do.

Passage Four: "Whoever serves me must follow me; and where I am, my servant also will be. My Father will honor the one who serves me" (John 12:26).

It's not that I have a deep need to be honored by God. In fact, I know what is deep in my heart, how much I need a Savior, and that selfishness will rear its ugly head sooner or later, but I also know that following Jesus in this life means serving Him wholeheartedly. It means serving the most important person in my life as I would serve Jesus if I could see and touch Him.

If you still think that marriage is 50/50, that you are doing your part and she needs to do the rest, then there may not be hope for you. If your attitude is less than thinking marriage is about both giving 100 percent (100/100), then you are going to get your feelings hurt sooner than later.

What if on your drive home from work, the moment you got behind the wheel, you asked yourself: *What can I do to serve my wife and Jesus the moment I've changed clothes and start to engage with my family?*

What does that look like?

It might be hugging the kids but then asking them to go play for fifteen minutes while you listen to your wife's day while massaging her feet. She likely hasn't had much adult conversation all day, and I guarantee you she has a need to have some. Serve her by hearing her (if you skipped chapter 5—or have already forgotten it—read it now).

It might be a phone call, asking if there is anything you can pick up. Serve her by saving her some uninterrupted freedom.

It might be an invite to take over with the kids so she can get out of the house to do something she has wanted to do all day. Serve her by allowing her to get away.

It might be simply getting the kids out of the house for an hour while she creates (or buys) something for dinner. Serve her by giving her a chance to do something that fills her tank.

And all of this you can do within the first thirty minutes of getting home from work! Just imagine what could happen on weekends when you have all day.

Marriage and family *is* about you. But it is not about you getting veg time every moment you think you need it. It is not about quid pro quo (if I do *this*, then she'll have to do *that*). It is about really remembering that being a servant to her, being her hero, does not stop when you get home from work. It may be just beginning.

Welcome to marriage. Welcome to becoming more like Jesus. Welcome to the most fulfilling and wonderful life you have ever imagined. Welcome to being her hero.

7

ACTION #5:
BE LIBERAL WITH TOUCH . . .
BUT NOT *THAT* WAY!

I t might be news to some of you, but there is such a thing as
nonsexual touching. It's not fictional—it is real. And guys,
there is compelling evidence that this crazy idea of nonsexual
touch can *actually* be accomplished. There is also a lot of compelling evidence that many of us men are not very happy about
it. Most men seem to favor sexual touching and would rather
leave the *non* part of touching limited to prostate exams.

In chapter 4, I mentioned that in many marriages, wives
are starved for encouragement and affirmation. Let me add to
that and state, in addition, many wives are also *skin* starved.

Behavioral scientists have coined the term *skin hunger* to
describe what happens when people are deprived of touch. For
people dealing with skin hunger, their skin is actually hungry
for affection—as in starved, famished, having an appetite for,
and desiring physical touch.

Guys, we can be pretty stupid about this reality. We think if we are having sex regularly that our wives are getting the physical attention they need. I used to be really stupid in this area, too, but I practiced and got better.

When Cathy and I celebrated our one-year anniversary, we had a significant conversation where we were reviewing our first year of marriage. Somewhere in the discussion she made the comment, "I wish you would hug me longer. You're not a very good hugger." I was stunned and displayed that emotion with a genuinely puzzled look on my face. She said, "I'm not talking about hugs that you're hoping lead to something. You're great at those hugs. I'm talking about nonsexual hugs."

Honestly, I didn't know there was such a thing. I interpreted every touch as sexual. When she would accidently brush up against me while approaching the refrigerator, I assumed she *wanted it.* (Remember, I was a newlywed—what did I know?)

Then she made a remark that sank into both my brain and my heart: "I'd really value some affection that you didn't assume was foreplay."

Ouch. She was right, and I got the message. Since then I have come to call this type of touch *affection without intention.*

I had to totally retrain myself. And I immediately began practicing. I would come home from work and make it my goal to hug Cathy for thirty seconds . . . without having a sexual agenda. It was tough to both hug my wife and not get caught checking my watch to see when my thirty seconds expired. It was such a little thing, but it became a big deal to Cathy.

And here is a bonus for all you horn-dogs: over the years,

I have learned that men who provide their wives with a lot of nonsexual touch often find that their sex lives improve as well. What's not to like about that?!

WHY NONSEXUAL TOUCH IS SO IMPORTANT

First, touch is important because it is a primary biological requirement for humans. Much research has been done about what happens when babies don't get enough human touch. Science tells us that if adequate touching does not occur during a child's first few years, there are a number of predictable outcomes when he or she reaches adulthood. Those results, such as diminished capacity for relationships and social skills, are not good. They are not good for the person, and they certainly are not good for a marriage.

On the other hand, when a person is exposed to an abundance of touching in childhood, it vitalizes his or her life, and this carries over into the adult years.

Face it—we all love a good back rub, right? Why? Because our skin thrives on touch, we respond with emotional warmth to those who touch us. Granted, this can be problematic (and outright embarrassing) if we don't know how to establish boundaries with our massage therapists. But when it is our spouses touching us, it's a wonderful thing!

From time to time when I'm at a restaurant, I'll notice a waitress put her hand on a customer's shoulder. Perhaps you've seen this technique too. Maybe it has happened to you. Have you ever wondered why a food server would do that? Is she attracted to the customer or to you? Nope. Not even close. Sorry to burst your bubble. The waitress touches the customer because research has taught her that the touched customer will tip more. Touch provides an *emotional connection* between the two, and it is often followed by a financial subtraction from the customer. It is all about the power of touch!

Phyllis Davis wrote in her book *The Power of Touch*: "Some people confuse skin hunger with restlessness, sexual desire, loneliness, or stomach hunger. We go to great lengths to satisfy our skin hunger without ever realizing what it is that we need. We attempt to satisfy it with food, with drugs, with entertainment; by burying ourselves in work, in talk, in activities, or with promiscuity. Yet it remains, this desire for the most basic form of communication—touching."[1]

Here, all this time, when you patted your buddy on the butt after he made a good sports play, you thought it was just a cultural demonstration of male camaraderie. Now it turns out that science tells us that you just like to touch and be touched!

Second, nonsexual touch is important because physical touch, as we discussed in chapter 3, is one of the five primary love languages. It is one of the key ways your wife feels and receives love and value.

Touchy-feely does not describe most guys. I understand. I also understand that many marriages are not doing well, and one of the reasons why is that wives are starved for physical (nonsexual) affection from the one whom they are one with. If you think of yourself as a man's man and the touchy-feely stuff threatens your manhood, I have this little gem of advice for you: Get over it! Now!

But don't go overboard either. There is a thin line between affectionate, nonsexual touch and sexual touching. And the truth is, guys are not very good at knowing where the line is. You might think it's sexy to come up and grope at your wife's important body parts. But I have done a thorough study of women, and 100 percent say that your groping does not turn them on. So slow it down, spanky!

Instead, hold hands with your wife while out for a walk. Rub her feet while she is watching television. Put your arm around her at church. Play footsies with her in a restaurant. Kiss her on the cheek while she is falling asleep. Rub her back when you wake up in the morning. All of these nonsexual touches communicate love and value. Her body needs it, but more important, her heart needs it too.

HOW HER SKIN HUNGER AFFECTS YOUR MARRIAGE AND SEX LIFE

For most women nonsexual touch helps them gain a sense of connection with their husbands. This connection leads to arousal. Men want to be touched in sexual ways. We don't need touch for arousal. We simply need oxygen.

I have told my wife that I am always ready for sex and that she doesn't have to ask, "Do you want to?" I tell her, "Just save those four words and start stripping! I'll know what you mean." Unfortunately for us, women are not wired like we are. For them touch is a vital part of achieving emotional intimacy.

For a man the ultimate goal of touching is orgasm! (Our own.) Here's a joke most men understand:

QUESTION: "HOW MANY ORGASMS DOES IT TAKE FOR A MAN TO SATISFY A WOMAN?"

ANSWER: "WHO CARES?"

For most women the goal of touch is not orgasm. The goal is connection and the journey that leads to it.

In the book *Intimate Behavior*, author Desmond Morris lists fairly defined universal steps from courtship to intimacy that appear in most cultures.[2] Though they have been around for many years, it's helpful to see them written out. These twelve steps used to take a while, but today the progression can move pretty quickly:

1. Eye to body
2. Eye to eye
3. Voice to voice
4. Hand to hand
5. Arm to shoulder
6. Arm to waist
7. Mouth to mouth
8. Hand to head
9. Hand to body

10. Mouth to breast
11. Hand to genital
12. Genital to genital

Here is the key to better understanding: for women there is an emotional involvement at *each step*, and each step *strengthens* her relational attachment. On the other hand, most men do not need steps 1 through 11. To them, they are not productive. Guys do not need connection. We need step 12 (a lot!), which is why the female gender often perceives us as having a one-track mind. You have probably heard the saying "All men are pigs." Regrettably for us, as with most sayings, there is at least a grain of truth to this one.

I go mountain bike riding with some buddies now and then. One day we were riding on the street before we got to the trailhead, and we passed a thirtysomething woman on the sidewalk. She was attractive and wearing what appeared to be her daughter's clothes. Think toddler-sized daughter. We all noticed her—it was impossible *not* to notice. Still, one guy in our group—a CEO in his forties and father of three—lost it in the heat of the moment and gave a good old-fashioned wolf whistle: "Woo-wooooooooo!"

Where did that come from? I couldn't remember the last time I actually heard a man whistling at a woman. As I said, we all noticed the woman, but this knucklehead's self-control disappeared—I think because he was with other guys—and he whistled at her. Can you say *jerk*?

Guys, when in the entire history of humanity has that

method ever worked? When has a woman been so flattered by a bunch of sweaty bikers or overweight construction workers who whistle or catcall that she stops, smiles, and says, "Oh, thank you! Who whistled? Okay, pal, let's forget steps 1 through 11; meet me behind the outhouse, and we'll go straight to step 12!"

I'll tell you when it's happened: *never!*

Men, we are faced with the challenge of overcoming the biological *oinker* within. (I believe that *oinker* is the Greek word for *pig*, but I could be wrong.) Women do not face this same challenge. For us attachment and emotional connection with our wives happens *after* step 12, which is why a guy can be in the middle of a fight with his wife and suddenly stop and say, "Let's just have sex, and we'll be fine!" For the male heart *the act* brings an emotional connection.

We need to get a grip on reality and understand that for our wives it is the journey through steps 1 through 11 that leads them to that twelfth and final step. If we avoid those steps, the connection and attachment are not there for our wives, the emotional intimacy is lost, and sex loses its significance for her. She may go through with it and "take one for the team," but it has little value.

This lack of connection, attachment, and intimacy is why so many couples become bored with their sex lives.

She says, "He doesn't pursue attachment and emotional intimacy."

He says, "She doesn't put out."

She feels "used" and disengages.

He becomes passive-aggressive and turns to pornography.

I understand that a lot of people might disagree with me on this, but besides the temporary adrenaline rush that works like a cocaine-induced dopamine fix, I believe the increase we see in married men using pornography today is directly related to their having poor sexual relations with their wives. Instead of working on one's sex life, it is often much easier to be quickly satisfied with porn. It is always just one click away.

If you are into pornography, let me tell you plainly: the visual affairs you are having may give you quick, immediate pleasure, but it is destroying your marriage. This isn't because your wife is aware of your behaviors (though she likely knows), but because you are settling for less than the best in your marriage and in your heart. Pornography is artificial sex. It's like filling yourself up on junk food when God has prepared a banquet for you to feast upon.

For the sake of your marriage, work on your sex life *with your wife*. Sure, you might have to eat a bit of your pride. You might have to admit that you don't know everything about sex or about satisfying your wife. But I've said it before, practice (with your wife) makes things a lot better.

Are you up for a challenge (so to speak)? I know of men who have committed to ninety days of sexual upgrade. First, they commit to no porn or self-satisfaction. They find whatever accountability they need, and they clear their minds, build new habits, and man up to purity. Yes, it can be done.

Next, and here's the tough part, if their wives are willing, they try to upgrade their skills. My better-than-educated guess is there are a fair amount of women who wish their husbands had more mojo in bed, more desire to focus on her.

Today's culture, in case you haven't noticed, is raising a more sexualized woman than it did twenty years ago. These women *sometimes* equate sex with relational happiness. They are not bashful about wanting theirs but get frustrated at a man's level of knowledge outside of hip movements.

What would happen if the woman were addicted to orgasm instead of you? What if every time you made a move, your wife knew that she was going to have pleasure even if you didn't? This book is not a sex manual, at least not the technical variety. But good ones are out there. If you think you know it all and don't want to upgrade, then fine. But if you are not convinced that one aspect of getting to One Heart faster might entail pleasing her first and always—at least to the point where she is convinced this is what you want most—then sex will eventually be a fading pleasure.

All women are different in this area, but the most unselfish aspect she will notice about you, if you really mean it, is in bed. Even if you are not a reader, books (not videos, men) in this area are actually fun to read [cough, cough], not that I have ever had to read one, of course [smile].

FINAL THOUGHT: THERE ARE DESERT YEARS IN MARITAL SEX

A mention should also be given about sex during the years the kids are between birth and school. Sorry. It's just not going to be what it was.

The key during these years filled with lack of sleep, bad-timing knocks on the door, and no money for date nights or weekend getaways, is communication. Just because *her* libido is down doesn't mean yours is. But it likely means that what was perhaps a two-or-three-times-a-week joy ride has suddenly become a once-a-week (or less) pity chore.

This is so normal it borders on the "expect this to happen, and if you don't, you're an idiot."

Find compromises that keep your head(s) clear.

Look. I get it! You want more sex. I know! I have you in mind as I'm writing this book. To a point, there is nothing wrong with that desire. But hear me out: ultimately, what you really need is a healthy marriage, not more sex. There is no such thing as a healthy marriage when your wife is craving nonsexual affection, emotional connection, and intimacy—with you—and when these needs are not being met. And there is no such thing as a healthy marriage when sex is all about you or you haven't mastered caring for her sexual *and* nonsexual needs.

If you really want to become more successful as a husband and improve your sex life at the same time, then get to work on creating emotional intimacy with your wife. Satisfy her skin hunger. Be liberal with nonsexual touch. Start offering up lots of affection without sexual intention. I guarantee you won't regret it.

─ 7B ─

WHEN LOW LIBIDO KNOCKS ON YOUR DOOR

I'd say this doesn't happen very often, but it happens often enough: sometimes it's the man who can't get his engine going.

With or without sexual or nonsexual touch, the "main part" just doesn't work like the *Men's Fitness* mag says it should.

Certainly that isn't you. But let's pretend you have a friend who may need help in this area . . . someday. By reading these few pages, you'll have some great advice to give him. You may save his sex life and maybe his marriage. You'll be *his* hero.

When a man under forty is not attempting to come after his wife at least a couple of times a week, there are likely things going on. Here are three possibilities.

One: he has something going on the side. Yes, I know this is shocking, but married men do this. It is potentially the most life-altering, soul-robbing decision one could ever make. He could throw his whole life in the toilet by one act or a hundred acts that takes getting caught only once. Either way, if he has something going with someone else, he is likely losing desire for his wife.

Two: he has something going with the Internet. We have talked about this already, but even a virile thirty-year-old is going to lose some desire if he has his hand on the mouse or is taking long showers every day.

Three: he has no idea why he can't perform, but something isn't working. Here are some libido killers:

1. **Too much weight.** Getting fat means you have managed to create lots of other places where blood supply is essential, usually your belly or your backside. When this happens, the blood flow river that leads to the penis is reduced to a tributary. Not only does completion get tougher, but desire goes downhill too.

2. **Alcohol.** It's a depressant, dude. It slows things down. And while it may have given you courage in your twenties, by the time your thirties roll around, it has the opposite effect of what you are looking for.

3. **Not enough exercise.** Back to blood flow. Exercise increases heart strength and blood flow to every part of your body. What is good for your brain is good everywhere else.

4. **Low testosterone.** Did you know this can happen any time after age thirty? And guess what? Lack of exercise, bad eating habits, and too much alcohol lower testosterone.

5. **Too much estrogen intake.** Google "foods containing estrogen," and you'll be shocked. They likely will be half your diet (especially if you're a nonorganic milk drinker). Yes, men need a little estrogen, but not a lot. When your body starts losing testosterone, it's signaling to you it's time to die. When you're old (or old before your time), the memory fades (it's the place in the brain where the blood supply seems to quit hitting), and with low testosterone or too much estrogen, things stop working in ways we'd like. Testosterone creams (and the like) can help restore your levels. But before you resort to creams or Viagra, get a blood test and your levels evaluated. You may simply have a genetic proclivity to low-T.

The key point here is *see your doctor.*

8

ACTION #6:
PUT YOUR PRIDE ASIDE

*T*ake it like a man!

Remember hearing that phrase when you were a kid? It was usually expressed when you were afraid of something: a vaccination from the doctor, a spanking from a parent, or a kiss on the lips from the grandma who had a *wicked* moustache. It was a manipulating slogan used when you needed a little extra coaxing to get beyond whatever frightened you. *Come on! Suck it up. Take it like a man.*

My dad would often use a similar phrase: *Shake it off.* I hated this one. I would come into the house, crying after being hurt playing football, and Dad would say, "Shake it off. Take it like a man." I replied, through my tears, "Well, I want to shake it off, Dad, but a bone is sticking through my skin. If I shake it, it will actually come off, and I'll be less of a man."

To see change occur in your own life and to pursue lasting

change in your marriage—the kind of change that will turn you into the hero your wife is waiting for—require some God-sized surgery that is not meant for boys. This surgery calls for you to *take it like a man*. It demands the little boy to sit down and the man to stand up. I'm not talking about physical surgery, of course.

Worse. Ego surgery.

Like a master surgeon, God is (more than) ready, (absolutely) willing, and (incredibly) capable of cutting away the cancerous marriage tumors that have grown in your life as a result of the years you have proudly chased after the cultural stereotype of what it means to be a man.

If you are like me (and I'll bet we're more similar than different), you need some major surgery of the soul that, frankly, *is going to hurt*. Unfortunately, there isn't an anesthesia for the soul, so there is no getting around the pain this will involve. Think of it as you would a vasectomy or adult circumcision.

Without anesthesia.

There, there. Calm down. *Take it like a man.*

I use the concept of circumcision because it is as much a spiritual concept as it is a physical one. Actually, there are dozens of references to circumcision in the Bible. God decided to use circumcision as a way to identify His people. In the book of Genesis, we read, "Then God said to Abraham, 'As for you, you must keep my covenant, you and your descendants after you for the generations to come. This is my covenant with you and your descendants after you, the covenant you are to keep: Every male among you shall be circumcised. . . .' On that very day Abraham took his son Ishmael and all those born in his household or bought with his money, every male in his household, and circumcised them" (17:9–10, 23).

Ouch. If you were snipped as a baby, you probably don't have the traumatic memory of losing your skin hat. If you do have that memory, I hope the cash that you dished out to therapy has helped reduce the emotional swelling.

The Jewish people revered the practice of circumcision. It was handed down from generation to generation. Fortunately, after this first batch of men and boys got clipped, baby boys were circumcised when they were eight days old so they were not old enough to be traumatized. But I've got to believe that when the then–ninety-four-year-old Abraham first heard the command to be circumcised from God, he had to be thinking: *Oh, God. You're joking, right? Really?! Noah got the beauty of a rainbow as the sign of Your covenant. Why change genres with me? What's up with having to slice my salami? That's so not fair! Would You consider the removal of the pinkie toe?*

I have often wondered, of all the ideas that were available to God (who knows everything), why did He settle on circumcision as a sign of His covenant? I mean, seriously?

However, God made the decision; circumcision was His choice. As a result, millions of Jewish males were circumcised to show they were God's people. Circumcision was their ID card. And as tempting as it is, let's move along and not think about *how* and *when* the men were required to display their ID cards (although I imagine there were some awkward moments trying to get into a Tel Aviv nightclub).

Fast-forward a couple of thousand years to Jesus' era, where circumcision was still used to identify the Jews from the Gentiles (aka *the non-Jews*). The apostle Paul (a circumcised Jew himself) talked about a different type of circumcision. He moved the scissors north of the belt line: "When you came to Christ, you were 'circumcised,' but not by a physical procedure. It was a spiritual procedure—the cutting away of your sinful nature" (Col. 2:11 NLT).

Other Scripture passages refer to this as the "circumcision of the heart" (Rom. 2:29; also Eph. 2:11 NLT).

God's plan for you and me is that He circumcise—cut away—the sin in our hearts, so that in time, we will look really different—we actually will begin to look a lot more like Jesus. You see, God's dream for us isn't about *something* we chase; it's about *someone* we become.

Circumcision of the heart means that God's intention is to form each one of us into the image (character) of Jesus. This means:

- less you, more Jesus
- less anger, more peace
- less self, more service
- less apathy, more compassion
- less condemnation, more forgiveness
- less pride, more humility

God, the Great Physician, wants to perform surgery that will heal our souls and change us into inwardly attractive men—into the husbands that our wives have been waiting for. He is able to make us *new.*

Here is how the apostle Paul described God's skill: "Each of you is now a new person. You are becoming more and more like your Creator, and you will understand him better. It doesn't matter if you are a Greek or a Jew, or if you are circumcised or not. You may even be a barbarian or a Scythian, and you may be a slave or a free person. Yet Christ is all that matters, and he lives in all of us" (Col. 3:10–11 CEV).

Physical circumcision doesn't matter in the new covenant. Your spiritual ID card is no longer hiding in your Fruit of the Looms. The Old Testament prophet Ezekiel predicted this change in the sign of the covenant, when he wrote: "This is what the Sovereign LORD says: . . . I will give you a new heart and put a new spirit in you; I will remove from you your heart of stone and give you a heart of flesh" (Ezek. 36:22, 26).

Through Jesus, your spiritual ID card is changed when you put your trust in Him and follow His ways with your life. We read about this in 2 Corinthians 5:17 (NLT): "This means that anyone who belongs to Christ has become a new person. The old life is gone; a new life has begun!"

Men, this is great news! When we humble ourselves and turn our lives over to be aligned with Jesus, we unlock the potential to become the men God intended. But like all surgery, surgery of the soul is painful. Do you know where the deepest pain is found?

It's found in giving up our pride.

Pride is a man's *headquarters* for all kinds of trouble in our lives: anger, conflict, defensiveness, selfishness, the need to win, the desire to be noticed, and the drive to prove our worth.

In marriage, pride is equally as ugly.

Pride urges us to say, "I don't need to change. This is just the way I am."

Pride causes us to blame: "It's *her* fault, not mine!"

Pride tempts us to claim superiority: "I know what the real issues in our marriage are. She's too emotional to talk clearly."

Pride is the F-5 tornado of relationships. Sadly, our wives are the mobile homes in our paths. Pride destroys more marriages than infidelity. Pride says:

- "I'm not going to be shown up."
- "I'm not going to lose this argument."
- "I'm never going to apologize for that."
- "I wasn't the one who was wrong here."

In case you are still wondering if pride is so bad, look at where the Bible says pride will lead you:

Pride leads to disgrace. (Prov. 11:2 NLT)

Pride ends in humiliation. (Prov. 29:23 NLT)

The fact is, when we put our pride on display, we actually prove how weak we are. Proud men are lonely, scared, and defensive. We will never admit it, of course, because that is how pride operates.

FROM PRIDE TO HUMILITY

When we allow God to circumcise our pride, something very powerful and attractive appears: humility.

Humility is the antithesis of the male cultural stereotype. Pride violently (kicking and punching if needed) and arrogantly races up the ladder to be the first one on top. Humility doesn't race; it takes a knee.

You might well be thinking, *I was not born to take a knee. I was born to lead, to achieve, to be the master of my domain.* I get it. But that is the *chase* within you, rearing its ugly head again. Yes, to take a knee seems so submissive, and guys don't like to be submissive to anything or anyone. Humility sounds wimpy and weak. Mel Gibson's character in *Braveheart* never took a knee. He painted his face blue and yelled, "Freedom!" Russell Crowe's character in *Gladiator* never took a knee either. He raised his sword and ran toward his enemies, yelling, "Fear my six-pack abs!" That's because warriors and gladiators battle, chase, conquer, and get all the hot chicks but never submit to anyone, right?

Think about it this way: when a warrior returns from battle and sees his king, he takes a knee. The warrior takes a knee not out of weakness but out of the understanding of *who* the king is. He willingly takes a knee and submits to his higher authority.

After a football game the coach calls the players together and says, "Men, take a knee." The athletes comply, not because they are weak but because they know the coach is in charge.

The coach has the wisdom and knowledge to help the athletes succeed.

Humility has nothing to do with weakness. In fact, it is just the opposite. Humility is a display of strength when a man fully understands that God is God. Humility flows from a secure relationship with Jesus, from the confidence that Jesus is King and Head Coach, and from the knowledge that His ways can be trusted.

Humility is heavy armor, and few men are willing to put it on, which is why it is such a rare character quality among us. Its rarity is also one of the reasons why women appreciate it so much and find it attractive.

If you allowed God to circumcise the pride from your life, how might humility make a noticeable impact on your marriage? Consider these examples:

- Humility enables you to keep your mouth shut when you are hurt so that your wife is not wounded by your counterattack of words and can more readily experience peace in her life.
- Humility is okay with using words that build up your wife and does not require a quid pro quo (an "if I do this, you'll do that" type of arrangement).
- Humility allows you to ask your wife questions. It allows you to listen to her without having to talk over her or have the last word.
- Humility allows you to choose personal inconvenience so that your wife can experience comfort.

- Humility rejects seeking eye-for-an-eye retaliation against your wife and pursues reconciliation.
- Humility allows you to say to your wife, "I'm sorry. I was wrong."
- Humility allows you to pursue conflict resolution with tenderness and resists protecting your ego.
- Humility allows you to say to your wife, "I've been a sucky husband. I don't want to suck anymore."

Humble men become masters at making others feel good. Humble men demonstrate authentic love. They have a way about them that allows their wives, children, friends, and coworkers to feel unburdened and unguarded. Humble men are likable men, whom others seek to be around.

We looked at what the Bible says about the negative outcomes of pride. Now let's glance at the positive outcomes of humility:

Pride leads to disgrace, but with humility comes wisdom. (Prov. 11:2 NLT)

Pride ends in humiliation, while humility brings honor. (Prov. 29:23 NLT)

Here is the bigger picture: disgrace versus wisdom, humiliation versus honor. You do not have to have a PhD at the end of your name to know which outcome is better.

Spiritual circumcision is elective surgery. God won't force

you to give up your pride. Still, let's be clear. God's desire for your life is that you allow Him to cut away the cancer of pride that threatens your marriage and to transplant humility in its place. Each man must decide whether or not he is willing to allow God to operate. The choice is yours.

If you want a healthier marriage, if you want a happier wife with a happier life, if you want to become your wife's hero, you must allow God to do His work, to perform His surgery on your soul. Your pride has to be cut away.

The Doctor's Cut

I grew up as a typical seventies California kid, where having a bronze tan was highly valued. Yes, we had sun protection back then, but my friends and I just thought it would diminish our tan potential. Instead, we used baby oil. Nothing conveyed "good tan" quite like the piquant odor of frying flesh. I was, literally, painfully ignorant. I paid the price then, through sunburn after sunburn. Now fast-forward to today. Well, I'm still paying . . . the price is skin cancer.

Let's just say I have a very intimate and frequent relationship with my dermatologist. He is a great guy, but standing before him in my underwear every three months while he scans every nook and cranny of my body, looking for skin cancer, isn't my idea of a party.

I am starting to get used to having him cut out my cancers. He makes a cut and removes some tissue and has it evaluated.

By examining the tissue, he can determine whether or not his cutting was sufficient (meaning, he got it all), or whether he needs to remove more cancerous tissue. The process continues until the margins around the tissue are clean and signs of cancer have disappeared.

My doctor rocks. He's got skills. He's got game. He knows what he's doing. I like him. I trust him. But you know what? The guy would have never laid a scalpel on me if I hadn't given him access to my skin. I had to invite his involvement in my life for him to make any positive difference in my condition.

I could have ignored my skin cancers, at my own peril, of course. The doctor would have never known. If I hadn't contacted him, it would not have made him any less of a skilled doctor. If I had not called him to set up an appointment, it would not have been an indication of his unwillingness to help. He was always there. He is there today. He will be there tomorrow. He is always willing to help. I just had to decide to humble myself, invite his help, show up for my appointment, and get near naked.

I hope that you see the parallel between my story and your own. Your marriage matters to you. You know it does. You wouldn't have read this book if you thought otherwise. Your marriage has an impact on your life every day, and you know it can be better. You don't want to suck anymore as a husband.

Sure, you can muddle through on your own and try your best to make things better in your marriage. To an extent, you will probably find some success. Hey, I can decide to try and cut out my own skin cancers too, right? I might get *some* of it.

But let's face it. If you could transform yourself into a better husband on your own, you would have already done it. If you had better ideas on how to become a better man and how to reform your character, you would have made those changes by now. The bottom line is this: left to ourselves, we don't have the skills to make the changes that need to happen for us to become the best husbands possible.

Here's the good news: Jesus does. He has all the skills needed. He's there for you. He wants to help you become a better man and a better husband. He knows how to help. He's the Great Physician, and He's on-call 24/7. You just need to invite Him to help, give Him access to your soul, and follow His gentle lead.

——— 8B ———

OVERCOMING YOUR
MAN MISTAKES

According to how I have arranged previous chapters, this is where I deal with your wife and *her pride.* After all, men don't have a corner on the ego thing, right? Women have pride and ego too! I should be giving you carefully crafted little points on how to work through it with her, and your problems with her pride would be solved.

Well, I'm sure there are women with jumbo-size egos who can't seem to face the truth about how their egos affect their lives and marriages. I just don't know many. And I'm not married to someone with pride who needs cutting down to size.

But I *do* know men. We all stumble in many ways. If someone would pay us to have an ego and throw our pride up in a defensive position whenever we felt challenged as men, we would be well-paid professionals. We could retire at an early age.

Monster-size egos of narcissists who can't empathize with others are reserved for the real big-shot professional athletes, politicians, CEOs, and a few pastors. (Oops! Did I just say that?) But pride affects us all.

We have enough pride loaded up in our buckets that we shouldn't be bailing out or pointing to the full buckets of others, our wives especially. God will bring them down and introduce them to humility as He sees fit. Everything seems to work out better when that happens anyway.

The key for us is what to do with our man mistakes. I remember one of my coaches telling me as a young man that mistakes weren't fatal as long as I learned from them. He then suggested these five actions:

1. Recognize your mistakes.
2. Admit them.
3. Forgive them or seek forgiveness for them.
4. Learn from them.
5. Forget them.

Good stuff! In competition if you can do all that in the space of about three seconds, you could likely be a pretty good athlete. And if we can do that with depravity in our individual lives, we won't get hamstrung by our own choices. Imagine taking care of our sins so quickly that we don't become prisoners to our past, left in shame and guilt over messing up *again*.

In case you don't know, this is exactly how it works in God's economy. John said it best in his first letter: "If we confess our sins, he [God] is faithful and just and will forgive us our sins and purify us from all unrighteousness" (1 John 1:9).

And it says nothing about living in guilt for months or years at a time. It says nothing about fasting and sackcloth and ashes. "Confess . . . forgive . . . purify." *Boom, baby.*

While our wives are not the Lord, a little humility and confession can go a long way toward getting the past back into the past. And this includes when our pride rears its ugly head and hurts the other halves of our hearts.

Sometimes I feel most heroic when I am apologizing to my wife. Why? It is the hardest thing to do! It requires massive doses of sincere humility. I hate to admit to her (really, to anyone) that I have (a) messed up or (b) allowed my pride to color my attitude, behavior, and decision making.

Overcoming man mistakes isn't just about not trying to make them. It's about admitting them when we do. And the faster we can do this, the better.

9

ACTION #7:
SHEPHERD YOUR WIFE'S HEART

In case you haven't noticed, this little book has been about draining out our tendency toward male selfishness and stupidity, and replacing it with husbandly selflessness and wisdom and heroism. And though I've talked a bit about behaviors that are damaging your soul within marriage, my goal hasn't been to chastise you for making every possible man mistake you could make. There isn't enough paper on earth to cover that list! And you can be guaranteed that my name would be right next to yours.

Thankfully, that list is totally covered by God's love for us. We know who we are deep down inside, and so does God. And if the Bible says again and again how much God is for you, even amid your sins and sin nature—that He is fully aware of—then who am I to clobber you for not being a paragon of manly virtue?

Hey, have you read Romans 7 lately and been reminded that the apostle Paul confesses his inability to do what he knew was right? He was a spiritual giant who wrote about half the New Testament, and if he couldn't win every battle, you and I can't either. There . . . breathe. Get comfortable in your male imperfection for a moment. It will do your heart good.

Our imperfect maleness is a state we will never be able to leave, but it is also a state we do not have to govern. We are subjects of this state, not the dictator. We have the freedom to not always live by its rules. We should always stay in the battle when it comes to soul-robbing behaviors that can bring us low as men, but the real battle is keeping our hearts close to Jesus. It is the evil in our hearts that sends our behaviors over the edge (Matt. 12:35).

There is another battle you should stay in as well: keeping your life and actions overwhelmingly tender toward the other half of your heart. Yes, that woman you vowed before God to love and cherish.

The title of this chapter may do one of three things:

1. Trigger painful memories, going back to when you were visiting your Uncle Willie's farm and that sheep chased you and you wet yourself (oh, maybe that's just me).
2. Make you skip to the final chapters because, *Heck, I can barely shepherd my own heart, let alone my wife's!*
3. Challenge you to a mission so important, so essential to marital success, that you will do anything you have to in order to be successful at it.

Stay with me.

A shepherd's role is to "look over." He looks over the flock entrusted to his care and protects the sheep from wolves. If you have children, you do this naturally and with full-on abandon—protection is part of your parenting instinct. Even if you are a mediocre parent, no one messes with your kids without consequences, right?

Still not convinced you are a shepherd? How about tending to the important things in your life, such as your car, golf clubs, guns, fishing equipment, garage, remote controls, grade school trophies . . .

See, I told you; you know how to *shepherd*!

To battle as a shepherd of your wife's heart is the most important shepherding job you have. And it is also the toughest and most complicated job you will ever do.

Women are different from us (to say the least).

Among other things, they are emotionally, um, *unpredictable.* They are intuitive (and right most of the time). They are way more nurturing. And if they have been wounded by life, they need healing.

If you thought marriage was just you signing up for working and paying the bills, getting occasional free sex, mowing the lawn and doing other chores, getting occasional free sex, keeping the kiddos in line, getting occasional free sex, finding time to get away to recreate with your buddies, and getting occasional free sex, well, you haven't been paying attention.

Learning the secrets of shepherding your wife's heart is often why God keeps us on this earth for so long. It is such a huge challenge; we need fifty-plus years to perfect it.

It's All About the Motive

If I were to ask you what are the selfish reasons you should work to shepherd a woman's heart, you would immediately know what I am talking about. So we don't need to go there.

Instead, let's make a list of some of the better, purer reasons to shepherd a woman's heart:

- She is more than worthy of the effort. After all, you married her, and whether you really grasp it or not, she really *is* the other half of your heart.
- Her heart is likely more tender than yours and can be easily bruised.
- The world and her mom or dad and junior high and a few boys have already done a number of things to wound her heart, so it needs strengthening.
- Her heart is one of the main reasons why you married her. It needs to be *looked over* and tended to.

There are perhaps a dozen other reasons I could list, but I'll cut to the chase. The number one reason to shepherd a woman's heart is . . .

- God wants you to help her blossom in every way so the world can see Jesus through her life.

Big mission.

This is not an easy assignment to make her come alive and restore and revive some of the wounding she may have experienced. But that is your assignment, and it's not to be considered mission impossible. My daughters are not married yet, but when they are, I will look intently at their future husbands and say, "I have loved and protected and nurtured Torie and Cassie more than any man alive. Now I pass that baton of responsibility to you. Your job, if you choose to accept it, is to take my job. Love my daughter more than I have and can. Shepherd her heart. Make her come alive as a human being so she lives the life she was designed to live."

I'll say it again. Big mission.

You have made it almost all the way through this book, so I know for a fact that you are a *word guy*. And if you play Words with Friends, you are *really* a word guy. So you won't mind that to help you with this assignment, I did an etymology of the word *husband*. (And since you know that etymology means "the study of the origins of words or parts of words and how they have arrived at their current form and meaning," I don't have to explain it.) Consider for a moment this metaphor: your wife can either be like grape juice or fine wine. It depends on how you choose to husband/shepherd.

The primary quality you need to husband grape arbors or tend sheep is *diligent, loving attention*. Those are the words that best describe a husband whose aim is to shepherd (husband) his wife's heart. (I should add *relaxed* in front of that, as no woman wants a husband who hovers obsessively.) If "the eyes of the LORD" (Prov. 5:21 ESV; 15:3) cover the earth, your eyes need to be diligent and loving to make sure your wife's heart is not led into places that will do it harm.

Another way to say it is, when the fine folks at the grape

juice factories want to crank out grape juice, they buy grapes, mix them with sugar and corn syrup and other wonderful-tasting chemicals, and quickly bottle the juice to make sure it gets to market as rapidly as possible. The grapes are likely of the cheaper variety, and the vines likely had little or no tending. Grape juice is basically cheap, colored sugar water.

Fine wine, however, is far different. And so is the process to make it.

A skillful and seasoned vineyard worker (a "vinedresser") carefully moves and shapes each vine on each plant as it is growing, being careful not to break them or bend them in the wrong way in the process. Why? So they will have the maximum ability to grow and carry grapes that one day will be turned into fine wine. Shaping the vines is his best work. He shapes, but then nature takes over (sun and water and soil and harvesting at the right moment).

But what he is doing is "husbanding" the vine.

There is no clearer way to put it. Your main job is to carefully *assist* in shaping your wife's many vines so as to help her be who she was meant to be, bending at the right time (never breaking) the most precious parts of her emotions and soul. As time goes on, she will bear the fruit that will be so attractive to others that those who see her will know they are beholding a fine wine, a wine with incredible value.

Okay, before you throw up your hands, close the book, and think me psycho, I have some good news: husbanding your wife is not entirely your responsibility.

God plays the biggest part in this whole process. And

though your wife also has a role to play, it is ultimately up to God to accomplish this all-important work. Yet . . . He has chosen to use *you* to accomplish a key part of this hugely important mission.

And *this* is the most rewarding—and hardest—part of marriage.

It goes against our egocentric man-nature to be so attuned to the needs of someone else that all we want out of them is for God to help them blossom and for them to realize how precious they truly are to Him and His kingdom. And in case you are not making the connection, this process is similar to what God does with us (John 15).

Which leads to the first thing you can do to come alongside God in this process . . .

TELL HER OFTEN WHO SHE IS

Everyone needs to know who they are. Throughout our lives, we are shaped by the things people have said about us . . . both good and bad. If a parent or teacher or significant adult told us we were good for nothing, that we just took up space on the planet and we would never amount to anything, we may have believed this lie. Beliefs shape our behavior and soon . . . *boom!* . . . our lives are shaped by a lie. Then if we don't think much of ourselves, we don't care if we abuse our bodies and spirits. Why would we? Look around; people everywhere believe the lie.

We all are the sum parts of what people (and God) have put into us. And most of those parts are either truths or lies we have chosen to believe.

You may not have any idea, but women are the most lied-to people on the planet. From an early age they are taught that their value comes in physical beauty, in being skinny or having high cheekbones. From parents to grandparents, from school friends to church friends, from TV to movies to magazines . . . all of it has told her—over and over and over again to your precious woman's heart—that she doesn't measure up. The message is loud and clear: "Who you are is *not* enough."

The same is likely happening to your daughter, if you have one. As an easy crier, I am brought to tears anytime I give this sad reality much thought. The onslaught of "You're not _____ enough" is a sad and sick cultural reality.

If while growing up your wife had what society considers a "physical flaw," a mom or dad who never convinced her she was beautiful and talented just as she was, a sister she could never measure up to, or boys and boyfriends (or a husband) who treated her poorly, her view of self may be seriously flawed. Even if she doesn't talk about it, you can be confident she has not been shaped correctly. Your mission is to shepherd her heart and help her change the course of how she views herself. How?

First, tell her every day she is beautiful. Sincere, well-timed, and crafted words are priceless. Speak words of love whenever they come to mind. When you feel them in your heart, say them. Don't hold back. Tell her truth as you know it with delight. Often. (Remember chapter 4?)

Second, look at her with desire and love. Convince her with your eyes she is worthy. Yes, do all these things with as much testosterone-appropriate maleness as you want. The world has perhaps broken her sexually in some way, and part of helping to heal the hurts in her life is to be "all in" when it comes to your passionate desire for her as your wife. There is nothing wrong with you looking at her, filled with passion *for her*. It is natural and biblical and beautiful, and don't let anyone convince you otherwise.

Third, most of the time, when she looks into your eyes, along with seeing someone who adores her, help her to see herself the way Jesus would look at her. I must confess, this is the most difficult of the three looks.

Consider this yourself for a moment: How would *your* life change if you actually got to see the way Jesus looks at you? He knows your flaws, your sin, your heart. Yet because He died for you, He can't *not* look on you with a love beyond your imagination. In His eyes even *you* are worthy of this type of love. Now back to your wife; certainly that tender feminine soul is even more worthy. Your eyes would communicate, "Jesus loves you so much!" Imagine what the woman caught in adultery must have thought when she looked into the eyes of Jesus (John 8). There are times when your wife needs to see how Jesus looks at her . . . through your eyes. Practice this skill. Master it. If you are filled with the Spirit of Jesus, you can pass on the love of Jesus . . . through your eyes.

I believe with all my heart that a husband can help shape his wife's life and help her blossom into the woman God means for her to be, as he is able to reflect the love of Jesus from his eyes to hers. As often as you can muster, she *must* see Jesus when she looks into your eyes. Personally, this is not my strongest of the three looks, mostly because I am more often looking at Cathy with passion (look #2). But here is what has helped me put this into better practice throughout the years.

I have embraced the journey of walking with Jesus daily and trying to keep in step with Him so I follow Him and resemble Him. It is by far the most difficult thing I have ever tried to do in my life. I once heard that a man will never be a good groom to his wife unless he is first a good bride to Jesus. Being close to Jesus is the best way to love my wife and kids. It is what I—what any man—must do for the other half of my heart. I will even go so far as to say, if I am growing closer to Jesus and being transformed by Him (remember circumcision in chapter 8?), I am more likely to see my wife the way Jesus does. Again, my intimacy with Jesus affects my wife, and this truth changes how I approach prayer, Bible reading, worship, and spending time with other guys who are walking with Jesus. These are not simply robotic actions to help me *look like* a Christian; they are actions that enlarge my heart *and* enhance our heart. She is the other half of my heart. I must do this . . . for her.

So if Cathy is not feeling and seeing that worthiness from Jesus (from me), will she feel worthy enough to become fully alive and give herself to others . . . to me? Will she know she is precious and beautiful and loved? It's all part of the package to shepherd her heart well. And speaking of her heart . . .

TELL HER ABOUT HER HEART

Women are smart and intuitive. They are glad when they hear they are beautiful to us, but they also are very aware of their physical flaws. Regardless of how many times we comment on their beauty, they likely hear it through a filter that has been in place for many years (*I'm too . . . something. Fat. Skinny. Pale. Short. Tall . . .*). Sadly, that part of what the world has done to them may never fully disappear. They may always feel a bit undervalued because comparisons are nearly impossible to erase.

But nothing can compare to a woman's heart.

Tell her.

Not only is Cathy beautiful in every way, but she also has the best heart I have ever known. Her way with our girls and son, her way with me, her way with God and those around her . . . I just love it. And while I could write an entire book just on the beauty and depth of her heart as an example to others, I won't. I don't want all the other women in the world to feel bad by comparison.

A word of caution: There is a reason I made this the number two thing you can do when you compliment your wife with words that come from your heart. Telling her the truth about her heart is essential, for sure. But I am convinced that telling her the truth about her looks *to you* and your desire *for her* may be even more important. Yes, she likely has been that bruised. And she just needs your words of truth to her in the physical area first.

And then . . .

BE A MAN SHE CAN RESPECT

Women can smell a bad-hearted man a mile away. If she senses deceit or consistent selfishness, she simply cannot respond well to your attempts at shepherding. The respect and trust won't be there.

What are a few ways to show her you have a good heart?

- Show her that you know what fills her tank and what sucks the spirit out of her day. If you are not perceptive or caring enough to recognize those things that drain the life out of her, she will not think you are wise enough to help shape her heart.
- Prove to her that you know where she wants to blossom. What blossoming does she need in order to feel God's pleasure in how she lives and gives her life? If you don't know that, you need to ask and learn. And listen! Find her sweet spot in life as to how God can use her. It may be far different from what you think. For example, you may think she needs to be in more social situations because she is so good with people, but she likely knows that margins and boundaries are needed to love people well, and so she can handle people in only small doses. Be a student of all that is her.
- Let her see that you are aware of the wounded areas of her life. You may not be a professional counselor, but listening, asking questions, never intentionally saying mean things that trigger her inner hurts will help heal

a heart wounded by someone else in her world (or past). Yes, God must be the ultimate healer, and certainly there are some wounds that we are not equipped to heal completely. But knowing what they are will go a long way in her trust and respect for you as a shepherd of her heart.

How can you do all this?

First, don't erode her trust and respect for you through a porn problem or some other addiction you can't break free from. Something like this signals to a woman, *Alert! Alert! I'm likely going to have to care for my own heart very soon, so I need to close it up to him and protect my own so he doesn't hurt it.*

We have touched on pornography a few times in the book, sometimes humorously. But you and I both know it really is not a laughing matter. It's actually a matter of crisis—it is the number one issue that I hear guys talk about at my speaking engagements. Pornography is always brought up. There are several great books about this topic, and of course, if you can't get free of porn's pull on your life, there are tons of counselors and groups to help you. Use them. This is one area in which men must lower their pride, admit they are not strong enough on their own, and seek help. And eventually win at. You *can* win! I have heard too many stories of victors, and you can become one too.

Second, exude *real manhood*, not a false manhood. False manhood is a house of cards that eventually collapses. If your manhood is found in doing things that men do at the expense of your wife and family, then you and your manhood are going to be awfully lonely one day.

Hunting and fishing and sports and cigars and Scotch and poker and working out to look and feel good . . . a reasonable amount is certainly fine. But if your manhood does not also entail taking on the hardest part of manhood—shepherding a woman's heart—then you have an incomplete and self-centered manhood that a woman cannot trust. Tough words, but I cannot say it any truer than I just did.

Lastly, become her best friend as best you can.

Find ways to share life and experiences that communicate how much you love spending time with her. Walking, riding bikes, camping, going to estate sales or antique shops, traveling, serving . . . whatever you both like to do together, do it often. This is how a man builds trust and respect, how he wins the right to be used by God to shepherd his wife's heart so that she blossoms to the world.

What a mission.

What a very difficult thing to do. And you thought your job at work was tough. Ha!

What a privilege!

——————9B——————

WHAT EVERY MAN NEEDS
SHEPHERDED MOST

I have made a few jokes about what we all think needs shepherding most from our spouses. It has been a virtual hunting trip or men's retreat, filled with sexual innuendo and machismo. Hopefully you have laughed a bit along the way.

But I really should back off a little and admit what we all know: every man is different. We go through phases and seasons, and all of us are not always thinking only about when our next sexual experience will be.

Having said that, most of us would agree that if we had all the passion we think we really need, we would be much better at shepherding our wives' hearts.

True that.

But that is not how it works. And there are really no guarantees that if you do a fabulous job at shepherding your wife's heart, she will want and do the same for you.

I *hope* she will, but I cannot with a straight face tell you it will happen if you follow any or all of the principles I have shared in this book.

Sorry.

But I do have a fairly firm grasp on what is right. And right in a marriage is to allow God to empty you, to fill her, so that God will use her in the world to bring light and life to those she touches.

This is Marriage 401, friend. Maybe even a graduate course in it. It is what *husband* means.

My sense, from what I have seen in marriages that truly succeed, is that if you are doing this for her with a good heart and the right motive, long-term, she will gladly do the same for you.

And if she doesn't step up to the plate as quickly as you would like, then God wants to do even more with your own soul than you can imagine.

As tough as it is, embrace this.

He really *is* about helping you be more like Jesus. And, well, Jesus did what was right because it was right. And He was more of a man than any man who ever lived.

I know very few Christian men who don't want to be the men God wants them to be. Deep down. As much as it hurts. As long as it takes. When we look at ourselves in the mirror, we truly want to say, "God, make me the man You want me to be. That's what I want most. Whatever it takes. However long it takes. Jesus, make me the man in this world You need."

To be your wife's hero, and in some sense to be God's hero on this earth, is to lay down your rights (as Jesus did) and let God use you to shepherd her heart in every possible way.

There is no greater job.

There is no greater joy.

My prayers are with you as you seek to be your wife's hero and be the man you truly want to be. I know you can do it.

10

AS CHRIST LOVED THE CHURCH

And now a final-final word as you seek to live out your heroic attempts with your wife. That one familiar verse: "Husbands, love your wives, just as Christ loved the church" (Eph. 5:25).

Again, thanks for letting me have a good time being lighthearted, funny in spots, helpful in others, and just to say stuff guys say when they are together. Hopefully, reading this book has been a breath of fresh air. And the fact that it's not a long book makes it even better.

But I do have one very direct, final, and serious thought to share with you before you put the book on the shelf with the many other marriage books your wife has purchased for you to read.

I have talked *to* and *with* hundreds of men about the Ephesians 5 verse. It is our True North as husbands, the passage we always go back to when we are trying to convince ourselves, rightfully so, not to be selfish oafs. What I have seen is that it works for a week or two, perhaps a few months, then . . .

Then life hits, and we fall back into that well-worn six-lane highway of putting the focus back on ourselves and off of the other halves of our hearts. Yes, our selfish nature strikes again. Yes, testosterone. Yes, the culture's barrage on our ability to keep our minds pure. Yes, the fact that work and sports and hobbies seem to keep us fairly busy and me-focused.

This book has fully been about admitting where we are, learning to think of our wives before ourselves, and trying to grasp what it means when Paul challenges us to love our wives in the same way that Jesus loved the church (His people).

There is an inexplicable tie Jesus had to the church. It was His body, remember? So He couldn't ever forget and *not* love it, and not want to give it words of wisdom on how to love and reach the world. He even gave His Spirit to help guide it. Certainly *that* would solve all of its future issues and keep it on course. (Well, mostly.)

I have a friend who truly attempted to love his wife as Jesus loved the church. I'll call him Rob. A good and imperfect man, like most of us.

Rob married young and waited years to have children as he and his wife worked through some issues. Then they had three lovely daughters. When he and his wife hit relational speed bumps, he remembered this familiar verse that was read and talked about at his wedding: love your wife as Christ loved the church. He hadn't forgotten it; in fact, he knew it so well he had it memorized.

He bit his lip and kept his mouth quiet. He struggled through a couple of decades of lack of intimacy, words that cut deep, and little or no physical touch. He truly thought loving his wife as Christ loved the church meant to never make her feel bad for barely attempting to meet his love needs. He didn't understand all of the dynamics of the marital union, but he thought he understood this verse.

And he was convinced that a man, especially a Christian man, lays down his life for his wife.

But there was one thing no one ever told him: while Jesus kept His mouth shut during the crucifixion, not calling on the angels to save Him during the worst of what man could press upon Him, off the cross Jesus taught against injustice. He had words to say on how to live and love.

Jesus wasn't silent all the time.

A married man will go through many seasons of laying down his rights, taking the high road, loving unconditionally, being the sacrificial one, and putting his own needs aside for those of his wife and children. As he should. Men *do* sacrifice for the ones they love. Heroes always sacrifice.

Sacrifice is one thing. Total silence is another.

Women are the most instinctual creatures on earth. They have a sense for things, an intuition when something isn't quite right. Face it; they are about fifty times more sensitive to the emotional temperature of the home than men could ever be. They were born with this, this . . . gift. And it goes way beyond knowing when everyone in the house needs to put on a sweater because they're cold and don't know it.

While we can easily admit women know and sense things men don't, that doesn't mean that we don't know anything.

We, too, know when something isn't right in a relationship. We may not always know how to fix it, but we know broken.

The point I'm getting to is this: if you have been married for five or ten or twenty years, and your love needs are not being tended to—over the long haul—then loving your wife as Christ loved the church does not mean keeping your mouth shut and dying a slow, painful marital death.

Seasons of sacrifice are normal. And if a child or the wife is sick or going through an overwhelmed period of time, then men, men who follow Jesus, *do* love their wives as Christ loved the church. They don't go running to the first thing that looks good to get their needs met.

But if your life has gone on for years and you know something is not quite right, loving your wife as Christ loved the church means you don't keep silent. At the right time you should appropriately and gently talk through your issues. You don't keep silent.

You see, God has given you instincts too. And if there are words or actions or long periods of love-need drought, you must speak up for your marriage.

Kindly. Directly. Lovingly. With every expression of unselfish words you can find.

Some who choose to speak up will be rewarded. A conversation or two or eighty will serve to bring the wife around to what is good for the marriage. As long as she feels heard as well, then compromises and new normals can be found. *Voila!* Communication really does work.

Others will be rebuffed. Her defensiveness will be evident.

It will hurt her. She may think you are being selfish again. She may justify her behavior in a dozen different ways. Hold fast.

If you have waited years to bring up your issues, you are likely not off course. A rule of thumb I have in confrontation is this: If you really want to tell something to someone, really lay it on her, then you likely shouldn't do it. But if you delay and ponder and are conflicted about it, then you should probably proceed, especially after months or years of prayer.

Sadly, a few men will go through this process again and again, and nothing will ever change. When this is the case, then loving your wife as Christ loved the church may mean creating a crisis. No, I don't mean a week with the guys in Vegas, where you don't tell her what you're doing; I mean a more strategic intervention, such as counseling. No matter how much you think it will hurt her or make her feel bad, if she has continually avoided change, it will be time to say, "We're headed in the wrong direction. I've tried to talk with you about it repeatedly as best as I could. I'm going to counseling with or without you. But I'd really like for you to join me."

Loving your wife as Christ loved the church never means silence in the face of obvious issues that are holding you back from pursuing the other half of your heart.

It means truly being her hero and risking her wrath or rejection for the sake of your long-term future. Few relationships can stand up in the wake of neglected love over decades at a time. My friend Rob's thirty-one-year marriage couldn't. And didn't. And the biggest regret Rob has is not speaking up at points when he instinctually knew something was not right.

The cost was devastating. Personal losses, his reputation, how his girls viewed him, self-respect . . . the price he paid was high.

And while I have talked a lot about sex in these pages, let's admit the obvious. Great sex does not always equal a great relationship. It doesn't hurt, to be sure, but some guys have a different side of them, where kind words, acts of service, surprise gifts, and quality time mean as much or more than physical touch.

Being embarrassed by hurtful words from your wife in front of others, having to do the cleanup details in the house most of the time, never being acknowledged with kind words or small tokens of love about your value to your wife all can sting as much as five years of a cold shoulder.

Whatever hurtful issues you are facing, if they are consistent over time, if you have tried to solve them to no avail, please, love your wife as Christ loved the church. Do the heroic thing and bring the issues to the surface. You will likely never regret you did.

————— Bonus Chapter —————

TIME IS WHAT MOST MARRIAGES ARE FIGHTING FOR

(This chapter is to be read with your wife. If she's not lying next to you, go get her. You both need to read and talk about this one together.)

I speak about marriage a lot! My audiences vary from crowds in the thousands to smaller seminars, from people who identify with Jesus to those who have heard His name used on the golf course only as an expletive. Following these speaking sessions, I hear common themes everywhere I go:

- "We are *so* busy!"
- "We just don't have the time we had when we were dating!"
- "We don't have the emotional intimacy we once had."
- "We rarely have decent conversations."
- "Physical intimacy isn't what it once was; we're both so tired."
- "We have no privacy because we have children everywhere we turn."

Chances are very high that the majority of couples are busy. The problem with a busy life is it leads to a busy marriage, and a busy marriage can quickly become an empty marriage.

How has the poison of busyness made its way into your marriage script?

First of all, if you live in a major metropolitan area, take a little guilt off yourself and simply admit that where you live contributes to your pace. Big cities (populations of more than 250,000) reflect a busy culture. San Diego, for example, doesn't live at the same pace as Dubuque, Iowa.

Though this lifestyle is not exclusive to big cities, if you live in one, you are always trying to get somewhere quicker and do things faster. And you don't see any real incentive to slow down.

Truth be told, of course, you can make yourself busy no matter where you live.

Fast cars going around a track is a very realistic image for today's marriage. Notice: they are (1) driving fast, (2) going in circles, and (3) living out the same script day after day.

Are you familiar with NASCAR? Not long ago I was invited to a NASCAR event in Michigan—all expenses paid. It was nice to be invited, but I would rather go to Chuck E. Cheese's with a gaggle of five-year-olds hopped up on Mountain Dew and licorice than jump on a plane to watch people drive in circles really fast. I told the guy who asked me I was "too busy" to go.

No offense intended if you are a NASCAR fanatic. I appreciate your passion for it, but I just don't fully understand your "sport." It is considered a sport, right? Someone once told me he thought NASCAR was an acronym for Non-Athletic-Sport-Centered-Around-Rednecks. I know that is dangerous to say in print because many NASCAR fans also like (a) guns, (b) hunting, and (c) killing stuff. So if you are a gun-carrying, car-loving, short-tempered NASCAR fan who doesn't have a sense of humor and is easily angered by authors who poke a little (very little . . . really little, tiny little) fun at it, I am sure that with a little time, coaxing, and Valium, I could learn to enjoy it, and you and I could be friends. I will admit, though, that it is more appealing than watching bowling.

Levity aside, NASCAR is all about fast, just like us.

In our culture . . .

- we have a bias toward fast;
- people who move fast are *busy people*, and busy people are viewed with prestige;
- busy people carry themselves with a sense of value and accomplishment.

Busyness is the new normal, and yet the cry I hear from so many couples is, "We don't want to live like this! We go to bed fatigued; we wake up stressed-out. It feels like we can go for days without any significant connection with each other." Can you occasionally relate?

BUSYNESS DISPLAYED

The effect of busyness doesn't *immediately* weaken your marriage. Actually, as I said earlier, it usually weakens you first; then you bring that weakened state of self—who is busy—into your marriage.

Busyness affects all areas of your life. You can be so busy that you stress out over which line to stand in at the grocery store. You don't want to wait in line, so you run mental algorithms for each line as you approach the checkout counter: multiply the number of people in line by the items in each cart, divide by the age of the cashier, and then multiply by the number of infants in line. Then you choose a line. But you don't relax; instead you keep track of where you would have been in the other line, had you picked it. If that person is still waiting when you get through, you yell, "Nice try, but I win, sucker!" and do a little touchdown dance next to the gum rack.

When you feel rushed and busy, you bring a rushed and busy heart into your primary relationships.

Have you ever had a fight on the way to church? More than likely you fought because you didn't want to be late. "Let's hurry and get to church," you yell to the frightened passengers, *"so we can love Jesus!"*

Raise your hand if one of the regular tensions or conflicts within your marriage script is over time. (Now put your hand down because you look really dorky with your hand up in bed.)

NOT ALL IS FUN

Busyness is also displayed in *less* humorous ways:

1. You lack personal depth—you become shallow.
2. Your relationships stay at the superficial level.

3. You experience an empty marriage because there is no time to give it what it needs to fill it up.

God gave me a tough question as I was pondering this chapter. Consider your life and the NASCAR metaphor. In your personal race of busyness, where is Jesus? Is He riding shotgun? Is He part of the pit crew, cheering you on to go faster? Is He in the tower, speaking into your headset, giving you instructions to do more and hurry up? Is He in the stands, observing your race?

Or could it be that Jesus has His eyes on you from outside the racetrack, and He's lovingly wooing you away from the NASCAR lifestyle that is putting your marriage in danger of crashing?

I think many of us are racing ahead of Jesus instead of following Him.

Jesus boldly proclaimed, "I came that you might have *life* . . . life more abundantly" (John 10:10 ESV, author's paraphrase). He didn't say,

- "I have come that you might be busy!"
- "I have come to bring you stress."
- "I have come that you might be hurried."
- "I have come that you might be overwhelmed."
- "I have come so that you will be too tired for sex."

I think we have created personal and marital scripts that substitute the promise of abundance for busyness.

Let's take a look at this promise of abundance in John 10: "The thief comes only to steal and kill and destroy; I have come that they may have life, and have it to the full" (v. 10).

Other translations say:

"My purpose is to give them a rich and satisfying life." (NLT)

"I came that they may have life and have it abundantly." (ESV)

"I came so they can have real and eternal life, more and better life than they ever dreamed of." (MSG)

The focus here is on *fullness*. Jesus says, "My presence is for *your* benefit!"

And we have Jesus' beautiful promise in Matthew 11:28–30: "Come to me, all you who are weary and burdened, and I will give you rest. Take my yoke upon you and learn from me, for I am gentle and humble in heart, and you will find rest for your souls. For my yoke is easy and my burden is light."

I think there may be an intentional connection between (a) the abundant life (in John 10:10) and (b) rest for our souls (in Matthew 11:28).

Some of you are thinking, *Wait . . . "Take my yoke upon you"? . . . I don't even like eggs. What's Jesus talking about here?*

"Take my yoke upon you" is a call to follow Jesus, to be

connected to Him, to be His disciple. To yoke oneself with Jesus is to *join Him*.

The yoke was a common reference to a wooden frame that fit over the shoulders of animals. It would harness them to one another, and they would work together, rely on one another, share the burden, and walk side by side.

When Jesus says, "My yoke is easy," He likely also is implying that it isn't tied to a fuel-injected vehicle. He's saying, "Come on, connect with Me, walk with Me, and see how My rhythm of life changes things."

These promises of partnership with Jesus and rest for our souls ought to be appealing to any couple wanting to stay connected.

But unfortunately, the promises intersect with our twenty-first-century lives, and we rarely have time to take Jesus up on His invitation, both personally and as a couple.

We are busy, and people are counting on us, right? After all, we have to stay connected to our hundreds of Facebook "friends," and see their photos on Instagram, and read their sound-bite wisdom on Twitter.

Some of us are so over-connected to others that we are actually under-connected in our primary relationships: (1) Jesus and (2) spouse. As a result, we ought to be learning that *busy* is the enemy of the abundant life, and *hurry* is an enemy of rest.

The first step toward rewriting the script as a couple is to connect with Jesus as individuals. If there is one thing I know, *love* in a oneness relationship cannot be hurried! What we want, what we long for, what Jesus promises can't be possessed with a NASCAR lifestyle and marriage. The marriage that is best for you isn't lived at NASCAR speed. You can't fully love when you are always in a hurry.

Jesus emphasized this slow-down moment when He told Martha that her busyness was quenching her chance at abundance (Luke 10:38–42). Mary had it right; she knew what was most important and sat with Jesus. I'm afraid that many of us don't have it right—we have turned life (and our marriages) into a race, when Jesus calls us to something different:

- We've been called to love . . . not run.
- We've been called to serve . . . not rush.
- We've been called to care . . . not hurry.

Love doesn't race. Love stops. Love strolls. Love meanders.

I am not suggesting a lazy life, absolutely not! I am suggesting one that involves more love and less speed. Slowing down is so counterintuitive to that which fuels our hurriedness. The faster we go, the more we get done. The more we get done, the happier (we think) Jesus will be with us. But Jesus' Great Commandment isn't "Get more things done." It is to love Him and others.

Before you think of your script as a couple, I want you to think of your own heart. Busyness becomes a marriage issue after it is a heart issue.

Most people don't want to confess to a disordered heart. We don't want to think anything is wrong or broken within that might be enhancing our pace and driving busyness.

Author John Ortberg wrote, "You must ruthlessly eliminate hurry from your life. . . . Hurry is not just a disordered schedule. Hurry is a disordered heart."[1]

Our nature is to try not to make it a heart issue; we would rather make it an efficiency issue. So we try to fix our busyness by simply adopting new habits in an attempt to become more efficient. We think, *If I can just better learn to navigate all my texts, e-mails, Twitter, Facebook, blogs, RSS feeds, and LinkedIn notifications* [I still don't know what that is], *I can become more efficient . . . and save me some time.*

Friends, please read this next statement carefully: efficiency is *not* the answer to busyness.

In actuality I likely need to become a little less efficient in my life, if I want to become more loving, because real love is willing to waste time.

Efficiency and time management are only the surface issues. If we stay there, it is like putting a Band-Aid on a hemorrhage. We must go deeper, and I have three suggestions that I want you to consider as a couple that will take you deeper. They are simple and practical ideas from which every marriage can benefit.

1. Pause and discover what's behind your yes.

That little word (*yes*) is what makes us so busy.

You've got to dig deep and break the surface of "Oh, we're just busy," or you'll always be busy! Here is what I mean by digging a little deeper—when Cathy and I pause to determine the why of our busyness, we discover the real issues:

- I struggle with insecurity. Insecure people want to be loved. Insecure people say yes easily because they want to please others. That is a big motivator behind all my yeses. I am a classic (and now recovering) people-pleaser.
- Because of my insecurities, I like saving the day. I want to be the hero, and wannabe heroes say yes.
- I hate disappointing others, which typically fuels my yes.
- Because of my brokenness (my issues) my first response is usually yes.

That's the deep stuff. And that's just *my* stuff. (Cathy doesn't have nearly as many issues fueling her; most of *our* busyness points directly to me.) As a man of my age (fifties) and maturity (twenties), I am embarrassed to admit this publicly—especially to those I don't really know. I don't even like admitting it to Cathy. But by admitting it, especially to my wife, it brings my issues from the darkness into the light, where Cathy can also see them clearly. When these issues are in the light, we see the struggles and can put them next to what we both value as a couple. Then when our values and struggles are clearly sitting next to one another, it helps makes our decision making so much easier. We can more clearly make decisions that align with our values.

The result: we can more easily say no to the things that make us so busy.

The stress we feel from being overwhelmed, busy, rushed, or hurried always points back to too many unneeded yeses (75 percent from me and 25 percent from Cathy; okay, who am I kidding?—90 percent me, 10 percent Cathy).

Our unneeded yes throws us into the NASCAR lifestyle.

Here is a simple but powerful question that every couple should get in the habit of asking one another: Why are we really saying yes so much? Okay, I exposed my issues; now it's your turn to dig a little deeper. (Start talking.)

You might say that you have noble reasons for being busy—it's for the kids! "Our kids play three sports, go to a tutor twice a week, church . . . We want to do what's best for the kids."

Great! That's honorable, but what if what you think is best for your kids isn't best for your marriage? What is best for your kids is a mom and dad who have some margin to rewrite the script so they can pursue a great marriage. What is very best for your kids is their parents having a great marriage. I believe the best way to really show your kids how much you love them isn't to give them everything but to give them the confidence that their mom and dad love each other deeply and have a solid marriage.

Don't get me wrong—it's admirable that you want your kids to be healthy and active. But what they need more is the security of their parents' healthy, growing, script-rewriting marriage.

2. Stop doing something every day, week, and month.

I want to give you permission to say no. Your yeses are hurting your marriage. Just stop doing something . . . anything. Practice saying no; you can do that—you have a free will. Say no. Get out of it. Take it off the calendar. Don't feel pressured to say yes. Silently protest busyness by saying no. Blame it on me if you need to. Tell the person that you are reading this really amazing book, by this incredibly handsome and fit author, who is so wise and tender and kind and humble, and is challenging you to say no to something every day. Then take a deep breath, smile, and confidently say, "I can't. No." Soon others will watch your life and want to borrow the book. Please say no so they have to buy their own copies of the book (again, blame it on me).

Why are you saying no? Because every yes is an invitation to busyness.

You can say no. I know you can. On the count of three, say no. One. Two. Three. [You: "_____."] Now, with conviction. [You: "_____."] Now in Spanish (it sounds better). [You: "_____."] Please give yourself permission to say no so you can say yes to one another and what really is most important in your life. Say it often.

Please note: I am not talking about saying no to the *easy* no.

1. "Do you want to try my mother-in-law's three-bean salad?" No.
2. "Do you want to go out Wednesday night and listen to my niece play the accordion?" No.
3. "Do you want to invite the Smiths over and watch *Here Comes Honey Boo Boo*?" No.

Easy nos won't impact your battle with busyness. Our real struggle is choosing between the really good and great options. The battle is that there are so many good options requesting your time, and discerning what is best triggers the difficulty. It would be great if your decisions were as simple as, "Should I pet this puppy or go get a colonoscopy?" Life isn't that easy and clear.

We have to learn to say no to some really good opportunities if we are going to say yes to *what matters most*.

I can sense some of your push-back: "But Doug, you don't understand . . . we're really busy! We've got so much to do that we can't stop!"

Okay, spanky, maybe you are not supposed to do all that you think you are supposed to do. Could it be that God gave you just enough time to do what you are supposed to do, and part of that time would include loving Him and those closest to you?

The most loving human to ever walk the planet didn't say yes to everyone. Jesus didn't heal everyone and at times had to leave crowds behind. And do you think that Jesus didn't have a lot to do? You try being the Savior of the world. Oh, wait! That's part of the problem, isn't it? Some of us are trying to be a savior, and that is why we are so busy. We are trying to be someone we are not.

My mentor often says, "Doug, there's one Savior in the world, and you're not Him."

3. Start rewriting the scripts.

You do not have to keep acting on a marriage script that is not working. Rewrite it! You are the only ones keeping your script from changing. No one is going to rewrite it for you. Let me get real practical here.

A. Begin with an individual rewrite. What needs to change within each of your hearts?

Friends, for some of you, your script isn't working. Everyone can tell it needs to be rewritten because they see all the . . .

- nagging,
- passive/aggressive behavior,
- temper flaring and other expressions of your anger,
- controlling behavior, and
- selfishness.

Play "what if" with me:

> *What if* you took Jesus up on His offer of (1) abundant life and (2) being yoked to Him?
> *What if* you walked with Jesus and learned how to live by His script?

Here's what I think might happen: life would become less about the pace and the chase and the race, and it would be more about experiencing God's compassionate grace. Do this, and you'll discover a new, love-filled pace.

Less NASCAR, more Jesus.

You work less at being religious and walk more with Jesus.

A friend of mine had this brilliant word picture that I have tried to incorporate myself. What if we looked at our actions in marriage—every thought and word and nonverbal communication—and played them out as if Jesus were sitting on our couches with us? It's another game-changer analogy if you deeply consider it.

If we were honest and really aware of Jesus' presence in our lives, we would live differently. We'd parent differently. We'd talk to our spouses differently. We may even watch TV differently.

Can you imagine walking into the TV room to yell at your spouse and Jesus is sitting there next to him or her? "Oh, hi, Jesus. I just came in here to nag my husband about putting laundry in the hamper. Oh . . . but . . . but . . . well, I've bought multiple hampers to make it easy for him, and he can't ever seem to toss his laundry into even one of the several hamper options I've made available."

Do you think you might talk to one another a little differently if Jesus were right there? Well, guess what? He is! He is present. Jesus is not a distant deity that you need to conjure up with a prayer so He'll come running to you. He's there. He's with you. He's listening.

To really begin to grasp how this theological concept can change your marriage, you should first consider your own script. What needs to change within you? I realize your first tendency may be to want to rewrite your spouse's.

We always want to make it about our spouses. "Well, he doesn't." "She won't."

Quit blaming, please. You are hurting your heart.

What if life wasn't all about you trying to change your spouse but, instead, about changing yourself? Your marriage would be so different.

B. Rewrite as a couple . . . daily.

What if I suggested that you give your spouse 1 percent of your day? Does that amount seem ridiculously low? Really, only 1 percent? What do you think? Is your marriage worth 1 percent of your attention? Of course it is!

$$1440 \text{ minutes a day}$$
$$\times\ 1\%$$
$$14.4 \text{ minutes a day}$$

Let's rewrite the script, where you two spend fifteen minutes of your day together—every day—face-to-face connecting. For some couples this type of script rewrite is going to require changes and sacrifice in order to find those fifteen minutes.

It will require one or both of you to turn off the TV or shut down the computer. You may have to take that stupid Bluetooth out of your ear in order to be fully present.

I'm not asking you to solve all the problems within your marriage—you have only fifteen minutes. I'm just asking you *not* to be a drive-by husband or a text-message wife. A commitment to do this every day will begin to get you somewhere.

Let's review:

a. Begin with an individual rewrite.
b. Rewrite as a couple . . . daily.

C. Rewrite our future script . . . weekly.

I'm suggesting you block out a time once a week, a more significant chunk of time, for just you two. Part of the time can be to talk about the essentials—the calendar, the finances, the kids, whatever. *But* you are also talking about your marriage script—and specifics of how you relate to one another and what might need some more intentional effort and taking time to update how your One Heart is doing.

Each time you meet, ask yourselves this question: "What is it about our script that we know right now needs to be rewritten?"

I think there is power in doing this once a week.

If you set aside this 1 percent of your week (that's less than two hours), you could easily change the direction of your marriage.

For some of you if you tried to answer that question

(what needs to be rewritten right now?), it would become overwhelming. The list of needed script rewrites is too long.

Here is what is great about doing this one time a week. What would have been a heated discussion on Wednesday—because she did something that bugged me—now becomes part of a deep discussion on Monday, without the volatile octane it would have had if we had discussed it right as it happened. Obviously, if it's a biggie, discuss it right away. But if it falls under the category of "things that bug me," save it. Who wants to live in a house when you're always angered? No one.

START rewriting the script:

a. Begin with an individual rewrite.
b. Rewrite as a couple . . . daily.
c. Rewrite our future script . . . weekly.

To really love each other requires time. Love always takes time, and time is one thing busy people need to find more of.

- Hurry races, but love walks.
- Busy glances, but love stares.
- Rush reduces people to a task, but love enhances people's value.

Your marriage could be drastically different if you looked busyness in the face and said, "No more! We're not going to allow a busy script to define us."

Everything in life would be different if you could hear Jesus say:

Less race . . . more love.

I'm gentle, humble . . . I will give you rest for your soul.

I have so much more for you!

I have so much more for your marriage!

Slow down . . . let's rewrite things . . . together!

One Final Thought for Couples: Please Read

In chapter 1 I talked to your man about chasing the wind, being so busy with life he didn't have time to chase you. It was a good starting point before diving in, helping him to become your hero.

But what if you are the one going Mach 10? Men are not the only ones who can become distracted by the busyness and pursuit of stuff.

The pursuit of stuff kills marriages throughout the land. It robs time and shared experiences but especially the chance to truly become best friends with your spouse.

Few marriages, unless they start later in life, start out with husband *and* wife heading out the door every day to conquer the world. Most slowly ease into better jobs, more money, more bills, bigger vacations and cars, and then they're caught. They become accustomed to their lifestyle, their jobs, their routines, and they simply cannot get out of that net.

What do you do, especially if you, wife, are the one caught?

While some women are natural thoroughbreds, racing from here to there, most are not. If you have a bent toward doing and achieving and getting things done better than most, you probably don't want to be stifled. Since you were born to run, you need to do so.

But even thoroughbreds need to have the reins pulled in once in a while, or they will burn out. And a thoroughbred from a natural bent is far different from one who is running for a temporal prize of more stuff. Only you and your husband will know the difference.

Here is what a lot of couples don't do often enough: every six months have an "Are we heading down the wrong lifestyle path?" summit. You can become so busy, year after year, just heading down the road you think you should go, that you don't ever stop, look each other in the eyes, and talk about whether it is all the right thing.

Here are some questions that can be asked during that summit:

- Do you love your job or just like it?
- Do you feel God's smile as you are doing it?
- Have we taken on too much debt compared to our income?
- What material possession goals do we have that ought to be put on hold until we can afford them?
- Are we setting ourselves up well for children and the need to give them the raising and attention they deserve, or are we painting ourselves into a corner with debt and work that we can't get out of when kids come along (or grow)?

- Is there a way to try going down to one income for a while and see if we can live and be happy on that?
- Is there a home-based business one of us should try so we can build a connected family lifestyle while still being able to afford our reasonable bills (emphasis on *reasonable*)?
- What are two jobs doing to our time together and our feelings of being truly connected as One Heart?
- What are three frustrations each of us is having, trying to navigate two incomes? Are those frustrations worth the extra money?
- Who are a few people we can talk to about our situation to get their godly counsel about how we are progressing in our lives, our jobs, and our marriage?
- Is there one couple we can find who could mentor us as we navigate all of these issues that could affect our marriage three, five, and ten years from now?

After you have done some of this type of one-on-one conversation, ask some deeper questions of each other:

- What does work do for me that nothing else seems to do?
- Am I working hard and long because I'm trying to impress or make someone love me more?
- What are our shared priorities about how we should be investing our time with each other and others?
- Is work a means to an end to pay living expenses, or is it the means to the end of buying toys and luxuries I'd like to be accustomed to?

- If God were to look over our schedules, what would He think about how we've chosen to invest our time? How we spend our money?
- Have we created a lifestyle that is so busy in work that we have no time for extended family, friends, serving at church?
- How long would it take us to back up in our work and lifestyle choices so we have more time for priorities we agree are important to work on together?

The key you are likely to discover in most of the answers is that one of you will feel strongly about some of the answers to these questions, and the other will justify or become defensive. This is the one sign you must recognize that something really isn't right. If one person thinks the other is working too much to the detriment of a shared value or priority, then that ought to be enough to start in motion a change of lifestyle.

Intuition and instinct, that gut feeling one has about where things are headed, cannot be ignored.

Ever.

And if one-half of the married heart says the other is pursuing life and work and money at a pace that has potential for a long-term negative effect on the marriage, then this *must* be dealt with sooner rather than later. If one thinks the priorities are heading in the wrong direction, they usually are. Don't wait ten years for the symptoms of these choices to cause other symptoms that will send the marriage spiraling toward divorce.

Men, this is your job, to make sure this doesn't happen

even if it means you have to trust your wife's instincts and change out that six-figure job that makes you travel, for one that pays less but keeps you home more.

I have seen this a million times. Maybe two million. Satan really loves it when he can put a couple on a merry little path toward the acquisition of stuff, throw a few kids into the mix, and cause the couple not to prioritize the marriage to the point of dissolution. Then he watches as the children see their parents fight and divorce, thus making their chances of having a strong faith something with small percentages attached to it. And when kids have little or no faith because their parents' "Christian marriage" didn't work, guess where that puts your grandchildren? Now your future life and legacy is shot to hell, literally.

Will you be happy *then* that you made a pile of cash and had a high-dollar home?

Satan is patient. He doesn't have to be in a hurry to destroy your life and marriage. In fact, it's to his long-term advantage to wait until kids can see it all explode and then blame God for it after it happens.

This reality is as plain as day. But even more plain is what God can do with a marriage if both husband and wife are "all in." If both realize that marriage isn't 50/50 but 100/100. Then children see what real marriage was meant to be. It's a glorious thing.

Afterword

The content of this book was conceived as a series of talks that I delivered to the Saddleback Church men's group. Given that I was on the pastoral staff at Saddleback as teaching and youth pastor for eighteen years, I had good relationships with many of these men. This gave me a wonderful opportunity to interact with the guys regarding the content I presented in the series.

Allow me to briefly review the content with you:

Your wife and marriage are worth your best effort—chase her.

Why? Because marriage is God's design and experiencing oneness with your wife, in marriage, is God's goal.

Seven Actions of a Successful Husband

Action #1: Don't Say Everything You Think

Action #2: Say What Is Powerful

Action #3: Don't Say Anything! (or Become a World-Class Listener)

Action #4: Go Big with Small Things
Action #5: Be Liberal with Touch . . . but Not *That* Way!
Action #6: Put Your Pride Aside
Action #7: Shepherd Your Wife's Heart

In the weeks and months that followed my series of talks, the main thought I kept hearing from the men who participated was, "It was really helpful and practical advice. I felt like for the first time I'd hear something on marriage and think, *I can do that!* But honestly, it was a little like trying to get a sip of water from a fire hose."

They are so right. Not many men have the margin in their lives or the energy to work on, at one time, *all* actions that lead to becoming a better husband. Looking at it from an all-or-nothing perspective can be overwhelming and lead to a paralysis that results in doing absolutely nothing. That's not good, and it won't produce the change both you and your wife are hoping to see. So here is my advice: Forget the all-or-nothing approach. Instead, start with trying something that made an impression on you as you read the book. The way I see it, doing *something* is always better than doing *nothing*. You can always do *something*!

Hear me clearly: you do not have to tackle all these actions at once. In fact, if you attempt to do so, it's likely you will fail, get discouraged, and stop trying. So start small. Take baby steps. Choose one action and really go for it. Practice that action until it becomes second nature, a part of who you are and what you do. Then choose another action to work on.

Look. It's likely that you didn't get where you are as a husband in one day. It took time to get that way. You drifted. Most husbands do. Recovery and change will also take time. It's okay. View the goal of becoming a better husband as a process. Becoming a good husband is not a sprint; it's a marathon. Don't give up. Persevere. In time, you'll grow into that superhero suit. Let's do this! Up, up, and away!

NOTES

Chapter 1: Stop Chasing the Wind and Start Chasing Your Wife

1. Max Lucado, *God Came Near*, deluxe ed. (Nashville: Thomas Nelson, 2010), 138–39.

Chapter 4: Action #2: Say What Is Powerful

1. Gary Chapman, *The Five Love Languages* (Chicago: Northfield, 2010).

Chapter 5: Action #3: Don't Say Anything! (or Become a World-Class Listener)

1. Gary Smalley, *Secrets to Lasting Love: Uncovering the Keys to Life-Long Intimacy* (New York: Fireside, 2000), 28–31.

Chapter 7: Action #5: Be Liberal with Touch . . . but Not *That* Way!

1. Phyllis Davis, *The Power of Touch* (Carlsbad, CA: Hay House, 1999; repr. 2002), 111–12.
2. Desmond Morris, *Intimate Behavior* (New York: Kodansha Globe, 1997), 74–78.

Bonus Chapter: *Time* Is What Most Marriages Are Fighting For

1. John Ortberg, *The Life You've Always Wanted* (Grand Rapids: Zondervan, 2002), 76, 79.

About the Author

Doug Fields graduated in 1984 from Southern California College (now Vanguard University) and received his MDiv from Fuller Theological Seminary in 1986. He has served as a youth pastor and teaching pastor for more than thirty years at Mariners' Church and Saddleback Church in Southern California. Currently he is the executive director at the HomeWord Center for Youth and Family at Azusa Pacific University and a partner at Downloadyouthministry.com.

Doug is also the award-winning author of more than fifty books and regularly speaks at churches and conferences around the world. Doug has been married to his amazing wife, Cathy, for thirty years, and they have three grown children: Torie, Cody, and Cassie.

More information about Doug, his resources, and speaking availability can be found at www.dougfields.com.

6 Additional Resources to **Improve** Your Marriage and **Develop** Your Parenting **Skills**

- Raising G-rated (good) Kids in an X-rated Culture
  10 actions all kids need in caring adults

- Should I Just Smash My Kids' Phone?
  How to empower your kids to make good choices and
  develop responsibility . . . without losing your mind

- Confident Parenting

- *Married People: How Your Church Can Build
  Marriages That Last*

- *7 Ways to Be Her Hero: The One Your Wife Has Been
  Waiting For*

- *Getting Ready for Marriage: A Practical Road Map for
  Your Journey Together*

Most resources include small group materials,
workbooks, and audio/video tools available
for personal use or group study.

For more information go to:
www.dougfields.com